Other Books by Elen Sentier

The Celtic Chakras
Walk the Celtic chakra spiral labyrinth.

Elen of the Ways
British Shamanism - Following the Deer Trods

Following the Deer Trods
A practical guide to working with Elen of the Ways

Trees of the Goddess
A new way of working with the Ogham

Merlin: Once and Future Wizard
*A personal look at Merlin in history and mythology and his
continuing relevance today*

Gardening with the Moon & Stars

Gardening with the Moon & Stars

Elen Sentier

MOON
BOOKS

Winchester, UK
Washington, USA

First published by Moon Books, 2015

Moon Books is an imprint of John Hunt Publishing Ltd., Laurel House, Station Approach, Alresford, Hants, SO24 9JH, UK

office1@jhpbooks.net

www.johnhuntpublishing.com

www.moon-books.net

For distributor details and how to order please visit the 'Ordering' section on our website.

ISBN: 978 1 78279 984 9

978 1 78279 985 6 (ebook)

Library of Congress Control Number: 2014956731

A CIP catalogue record for this book is available from the British Library.

Design: Stuart Davies

Printed and bound by CPI Group (UK) Ltd, Croydon, CR0 4YY, UK

We operate a distinctive and ethical publishing philosophy in all areas of our business, from our global network of authors to production and worldwide distribution.

CONTENTS

Acknowledgements and Dedications

This book would not have been possible without the support and encouragement of my husband and fellow gardener, Paul König, and my father, Joe Pennington Mellor, and my Uncle Percy who, between them, grounded me in gardening from the age of two.

I must also give particular thanks to several people without whom, again, I wouldn't have been able to write it. They are ...

The Biodynamic Association, of which I'm a part and which is a marvellous group of people who support each other in the work and make the preparations which are vital to biodynamics.

Jody Scheckter, Laverstoke Park Farm, whose wonderful work for making biodynamics available through his principles of Good Soil = Good Grass = Good Quality Animals = Better Tasting Food = Happy People! are basic to good living.

And lastly there's my editor, Dominic James, book designer Stuart Davies and cover designer Nick Welch, and all at John Hunt Publishing without whom it would never have happened.

About Elen Sentier

Elen Sentier is a writer, artist and gardener. She lives with her husband and cats in the Welsh Marches in a lovely old farmhouse where Biodynamic gardening is one of her passions.

Their beautiful fruit, vegetable and flower garden is Demeter certified and they are members of the Biodynamic Association in Britain. She and her husband have been gardening biodynamically since 1990. She also trained at Pershore College and has been gardening all her life. Her father and one of her uncles were keen gardeners who passed on their knowledge and expertise.

Elen does all she can to promote biodynamics. In 2004/5/6 she built medal winning gardens at the Royal Horticultural Society's international Hampton Court Palace Flower Show with the sponsorship help of Weleda and Dr Hauschka Skin Care.

For more about Elen go to http://elensentier.co.uk

Chapter 1

What is Biodynamics?

Biodynamics is using a set of eight preparations (the BD preps) made from vegetable/herbal, animal and mineral compounds to enhance the soil and the plants.

Biodynamics is also about working in harmony with Nature rather than trying to force nature to conform to some human idea. It's about learning more of how she works – after all she's been at it a lot longer than there've been humans around

Scientists estimate that humans branched off from their common ancestor with chimpanzees about 5–7 million years ago. Several species and subspecies of *Homo* evolved and are now extinct. Archaic *Homo sapiens* evolved between 400,000 and 250,000 years ago – a mere spit in terms of the age of the Earth which has been determined to be 4.54 billion years. So Mother Earth has lived eleven thousand, three hundred and fifty times as long as there have been humans on the planet ... a mind-boggling thought! You realise she must know her job of weaving the strands of Life together rather better than we do.

Agriculture – manipulating the Earth to get our food – is at most 10,000 years old. China and Japan are thought to be the earliest known agriculturalists, nineteen thousand years old, but even this is nothing to the 4.5 *billion* years the Earth has existed.

Its beginnings took place in the Fertile Crescent of the Middle East about 10,000 years ago and spread outwards from there into Europe. The diverse climate and major climatic changes in the region encouraged the evolution of many annual plants which produce more edible seeds than perennial plants – under-standably, as they need to reproduce themselves every year. These region's edible plants were available for early experiments in cultivation. Most importantly, the Fertile Crescent possessed the wild progenitors of the eight Neolithic founder crops important in early agriculture – the wild progenitors to emmer wheat, einkorn, barley, flax, chick pea, pea, lentil, bitter vetch. As well, four of the five most important species of domesticated animals – cows, goats, sheep, and pigs – lived there. The fifth species, the horse, lived nearby. As a result, the Fertile Crescent is famous for sites related to the origins of agriculture. The western zone around the Jordan and upper Euphrates rivers gave rise to the first known Neolithic farming settlements which date to around 9,000 BCE. We humans, and our farming, have been around for hardly a mere spit in time, it is well worth learning from our very experienced Mother.

Gardening with the Moon & Stars – Biodynamics (BD) – is about learning to work with the Earth's cycles. I've found this fascinating even if I don't understand *why* the cycles work. But then, I don't know why lots of things happen, like electricity, gravity and the weather. I know how to turn the light-switch on, I can read weather charts, I can appreciate gravity but I don't know *why* these things happen. Nor, I suspect does anyone else. They know *how* to make them happen, how to make electricity, how to read the signs for the weather. They have ideas and theories (a posh word for a guess) but their proofs are largely experiential and run on the lines of nobody's proved them wrong yet. That's quite OK, I can live with that. My gardening methods are much the same.

We use the BD Preps (biodynamic preparations) in time and rhythm with the cycles of the Earth, the moon and the constellations with the help of the star calendar – more on all this later - so we garden with the Moon and Stars.

Biodynamic gardeners use very limited external inputs – no chemicals or bought-in fertilisers, just re-cycling garden and kitchen waste through the compost, with maybe a bit of sand, gypsum, lime and some animal manure not available in the garden. So biodynamics has a low impact on the environment.

And the quality of the produce is enhanced. The superior colour, fragrance and good health of trees, shrubs, flowers and vegetables, as well as the latter's flavour and keeping quality, all show very quickly when you work biodynamically.

Biodynamics can be applied to any organic garden or horticultural project, including no-dig and permaculture. It's very practical, anyone can do it without having to know all the philosophy behind it although many people find they want to know more ... once they've seen the results of doing it.

The Biodynamic Method Includes ...

- Using the horn manure spray, **Prep 500**, to stimulate biological activity in the soil and improve the transference and retention of nutrients provided in the soil itself as well as that added through animal manure and vegetable compost.
- Using the horn silica spray, **Prep 501**, to stimulate the parts of the plant that you wish to use or work with – e.g. rose or cauli *flowers*, lettuce or hosta *leaves*, beet*roots*, holly *berries* or tomato *fruits* – to come to their full potential.
- Composting all organic waste products and enhancing this compost by adding the 6 compost preparations. This includes adding them to manure heaps, local authority waste, leaf mould and your own kitchen waste, as well as vegetable and weed compost.
- Converting from chemical pest and weed control to biodynamic methods to discourage them, along with prevention strategies based on good plant nutrition and careful cultivar selection.

Biodynamics is a *systems approach* where the garden, allotment, nursery or other horticultural undertaking is viewed as a living whole – similar to the Gaia Principle of James Lovelock – in which each activity affects the others. You put the preparations on the soil and plants, and into the compost heap, in time with the rhythms of the Earth, Moon and Stars, which you can easily check using the star calendar (see chapter). You also use your own observations – each garden is individual so, within the basic parameters of biodynamics, you adjust yourself to suit your own land. This produces strong and healthy plants in a healthy, well-structured soil that is rich in humus and high in biological activity ... all prerequisites for any sustainable horticultural system.

Over eighty years, since 1924, worldwide experience with Biodynamics (BD) has shown that these soil qualities can be encouraged, *and* degradation reversed, by BD techniques. Up to now, it's been mostly used in farming but the time is ripe for gardeners and horticulturalists to get going with it as well. Although animal manure has to be brought in, unless you live on a farm, the techniques still work excellently well in gardens, as our own garden here at Archenland shows. There are already many excellent organic gardeners out there, now let's use biodynamics to really make the soil sing.

Pest and disease control is generally managed by developing the garden as a complete organism that is in balance with itself and its surroundings – the Gaia Principle again. However, BD recognizes that things do go out of kilter now and again and enables gardeners to make use of specific substances for weed and pest control, made from the weeds and pests themselves. Weeds and pests, as you may already know, are useful indicators of imbalances in and between soil and plants. If you know what the weeds and pests are telling you about the state of the soil you can work on the cause rather than putting a sticking plaster over the resulting hurt.

I often say biodynamics is good organic practice with added oomph.

The oomph is added through the Preparations. They are *fundamental* to biodynamics. They are used in conjunction with,

4

not instead of, good established organic practices such as composting, manuring and crop rotations. The Preparations work directly with the dynamic, biological processes of the soil and with the cycles, which are the basis of soil fertility, as well as with the growing plants themselves.

The Preparations are *not* fertilisers in themselves but they greatly assist the whole growth process. As such, they only need to be used in very small amounts a few times a year, so going biodynamic isn't going to mean you have no time for anything else!

How did biodynamics come about? Biodynamics is the oldest organised form of organic gardening and agriculture. It was concern about the worrying trends developing in agriculture that led farmers to ask Rudolf Steiner to give his 'Agriculture Lectures" in 1924, on which the biodynamic agricultural movement is founded. The farmers' concerns were ...

- increasing mechanisation of agriculture
- a sense that nature is becoming degraded, losing its vitality
- pollution of the environment
- signs of illness in trees
- violent changes in the weather

It seems nothing is new.

The farmers' concerns resulted in the series of eight lectures that Steiner gave at the house of his friend Count Keiserling. The lectures began a movement which now spans the world. Australia, New Zealand, South Africa, India, Europe, Ireland, the UK and the USA all have very strong biodynamic movements and I've recently had enquiries from Japan. It seems that Poland has chosen to make its government-supported agriculture biodynamic. Biodynamics is particularly prominent in wine-making where such experts as Oz Clarke say biodynamic wine is the best wine they have ever tasted. Many famous chefs also prefer to use biodynamic produce.

So biodynamics is not a "weirdo, long-hair and sandals brigade" thing. Nor is it some bizarre magical pseudoscience. It's true that we may not be able to explain everything about it as fully as we can, say, bread-making or steel production but ... have you ever tried to say "why" (not how) electricity works? And physics comes up with wonderful apparent paradoxes like "is light waves or particles, or both?" We seem quite able to cope with not having a complete scientific knowledge of these things. Perhaps experiencing the pleasures of biodynamics, seeing the beautiful plants, eating the good food, drinking the excellent wine, will help us overcome our doubts and fears of this well established form of growing.

Who was Rudolf Steiner? He was a Croatian doctor of philosophy from the University of Rostock. He spent his life researching many subjects and is perhaps best known for his pioneering work in education which has resulted in the Waldorf Schools, begun in 1919. He began the Anthroposophical Society in 1923. His last piece of work in a very busy life was founding the biodynamics movement in 1924. Steiner's philosophy is about people, how they do things best, how to encourage this and how to work in harmony with nature. Wikipedia has a good section on him if you want to read more and there are various web sites. Steiner House in London is the home of the Anthroposophical Society and you will find all his work there. They are on the web and do a mail-order library if you want to borrow the books. They also run all sorts of workshops.

The Eight Biodynamic Preparations ...

Spray Preparations: 500 & 501
Preparation 500: HORN MANURE. This enlivens the soil,

increasing the microflora and mycorrhiza so increasing the availability of nutrients and trace elements and making them available to the plants. This *availability* is key to plant growth. There may be lots of nutrients in the soil but if the plant can't absorb them then they might as well not be there, the plant starves. The horn manure preparation also helps root growth, in particular the fine root hairs that are essential for the plant to take up water and nutrients. It also helps and increases humus formation of the soil itself, as well as improving the soil's structure and water holding capacity.

Preparation 501: HORN SILICA. This helps the plant to come to its full potential – such as a flower, tree, fruit or vegetable – and so have better form, colour, aroma, flavour and, for vegetables and fruit, better nutritional quality.

Compost Preparations: 502 to 507

- 502 – Yarrow *Achillea millefolium*
- 503 – Chamomile *Chamomilla metrecaria recutita*
- 504 – Nettle *Urtica dioica*
- 505 – Oak bark *Quercus robur*
- 506 – Dandelion *Taraxacum officianale*
- 507 – Valerian *Valeriana officianalis*

These increase the humification so helping the cation exchange (more about these later). These help the dynamic cycles of the macro- and micro- flora and fauna in the compost heap, so increasing the nutrients formed in the composting process as well as its structure and water-holding capacity. This helps the whole garden.

How Doing Biodynamics Can Help You

- The preparations increase the soil biology to work for you
- Using the preps naturally creates deeper topsoil – *this really happens, it's one of the things that convinced me*

- The water holding capacity increases, helping both drought and flood – *we see that in the garden here, especially now climate change has set in*
- Plant health, beauty and yield improves
- Weeds and pests are reduced to easily manageable levels
- The beneficial animals and insects are encouraged to live in your garden
- You don't have to spend lots of money at garden centres every year on compost, chemical fertilisers or pest controls
- Working with the rhythms of the Earth, Moon and Stars optimises the plant growth-cycles so vegetables and flowers look, smell and taste good, and keep longer
- The garden quickly looks and feels gorgeous, so you feel good too
- Far less stress – everything works with you
- Low impact on the environment through limited external inputs

Biodynamics is easy ... I want to say this right from the beginning. It does *not* mean you have to spend many hours making strange brews *or* spend loads of money. You can buy all the preparations, ready to stir, from your local or national biodynamic association – see Contacts. You buy a star calendar from Amazon as well as your local BD association too, to show you *when* to do *what*. The likely cost for the calendar and a year's supply of preps for the average-size town garden is probably going to be under £25 – less than 50p a week.

This book shows you how you too can work this way – easily and without having to take on any strange philosophies.

Actually using the eight preparations, *in conjunction with the star calendar*, is what biodynamics is about; using the preparations is the corner-stone of biodynamics. It's about getting the preparations on the ground, on the plants and in the compost heap; this is what does the magic.

Added to good organic practice, the preparations increase soil and plant health and vitality, enhance colour, form, fragrance and flavour as well as helping plants resist pests and diseases.

There are two types of preparation – the Spray preparations and the Compost preparations.

The **spray** preparations that are used directly on the soil and plants; they are made using a cow's horns as the container and are sometimes known as the "horn preps".

The **compost** preparations that (as their name suggests) work in the compost heap. They are made in all sorts of things and are more complex to make. *How* they are made is dealt with in the chapter Making the Preparations but *you* don't need to do this unless you wish to. All the preps are available for sale, cheaply, through your national biodynamic association.

What you have to do is turn them into a form that the soil and plants can use.

We are going to work first with the two spray preparations. They are the easiest to use and the ones your land needs you to begin with. With both horn manure (500) and horn silica (501) you do this by stirring a very small portion of whichever you need in a bucket of water for an hour, on the right day and time of the month according to the star calendar. You then spray it onto either the soil (Prep 500) or the relevant plant (Prep 501) so doing the magic.

For this, you need the **Star Calendar**. You can get one easily and cheaply from Amazon and it would be useful to get one now so you can look at it as you read this chapter.

Chapter 2

The Star Calendar

"Planting by the Moon" is quite well known but biodynamics is far more than the phases of the moon. In BD we see the moon as a lens that focuses the energies of each of the twelve constellations (of stars) onto the Earth as she passes in front of them during her 28 day period each month.

Maria Thun (followed now by her son, Mathias) is the pioneer of the Star Calendar. Her approach is entirely practical and based on over fifty years of experiment and scientific observation. In the 1950s she began the research that built the calendar by carrying out experiments to attempt to establish a connection between the growth of plants and the movements of the stars. Her first experiment was to sow a plot of radishes every day for an entire growing season and observe the performance of each sowing. She discovered four very noticeable differences in the plots.

Some produced larger roots; this happened when the seeds

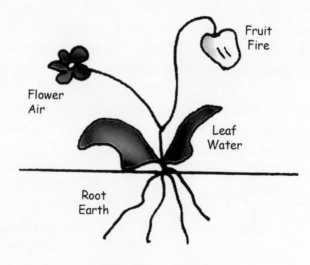

Fig 1: Parts of a Plant

were sown when the moon was focusing the Earth constellations, bull, virgin and goat. Those sown in Water constellations, fishes, crab and scorpion had larger leaves. Those sown in Air constellations, waterman, twins and scales produced more flowers. And the fourth group went more quickly to seed, having been sown in Fire constellations, ram, lion and archer.

Thun deduced that sowing the seeds in the four separate categories of constellation – earth, water, air and fire – had a direct effect on which part of the plant grew best. And she saw that each category of constellation had a particular effect on one part of the plant.

Further work showed Thun that it made a difference which half of the month things were sown in as well. This made her realise that the moon did different things depending on whether she is on a rising arc – rising higher in the sky each night – or on a descending arc – rising lower in the sky each night. From this, Thun remembered the old farmers' almanacs that talked about "moon riding high" and "moon riding low" and realised the old folk knew a thing or two about this cycle. The results of this research are what we call the Breathing Cycles – see later in this chapter.

This research was the beginning of the star calendar. Thun and her son did a massive amount of scientific research into biodynamic growing and updates the calendar each year with the latest findings.

This is why we call it the **star calendar** – because the *moon* focuses the energy of the *stars*. Without the star calendar we wouldn't know *when* to apply the preparations.

Thun's calendar is set in GMT, Greenwich Mean Time, on which all other time is based. Biodynamic associations in other countries produce their own calendars which give the times as they are in those countries. This makes them easier to use than translating GMT into local time.

The *primary* function of the star calendar is to show you when to apply the preparations.

Its *secondary* function shows the most advantageous times for:

- **sowing** – all seeds you start in pots, and/or soak in water *as well as* those you sow directly into the ground
- **planting** – including planting out annual and herbaceous plants either bought in from garden centres or grown on by you from seed or plugs; planting shrubs and trees, bare-root and potted, grown by you or from a nursery or plant centre; *and* planting out your vegetables after germinating them in pots
- **cultivation** – weeding, thinning, pruning, feeding, mulching
- **harvest** – cutting flowers, picking fruit and vegetables

The star calendar may appear confusing at first but once you've worked with it for a month it gets much easier.

Some biodynamic practitioners can get so wordy about astrological thingamajigs that it can boil one's brain. You really don't need to boil your brain to do biodynamics, it isn't that hard and Steiner certainly never intended it to be! There are a few things to get your head around first so we'll go slowly through them and make things as obvious as possible.

The Moon

The star calendar works with more than just the Moon phases. The moon focuses the energy of each of the star constellations as she travels around the Earth once every 28-29 days. She does this as she passes in front of each of the constellations.

As she passes in front of each constellation, the moon focuses the energy from the stars in that constellation onto the Earth. This gives the days when it's best to work with each part of the plant; each constellation carries the energy relevant to that part of the plant. The following table shows the correspondences between

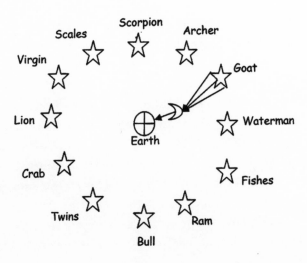

Fig 2: Moon as Lens

the parts of the plant and the constellations.

Root	Leaf	Flower	Fruit
Earth	*Water*	*Air*	*Fire*
Bull	Fishes	Waterman	Ram
Virgin	Crab	Twins	Lion
Goat	Scorpion	Scales	Archer

In the star calendar each day has the moon in front of one of these constellations and so is called a Root, Leaf, Flower or Fruit day, signifying the part of the plant you want to work with.

Breathing Cycles

Many of us who work biodynamically, growing plants and gardening, use the term "breathing cycles" as the most descriptive analogy for what our observations show us is happening. I am not saying the Earth literally breathes (I don't know if she does or not) but what happens is best described as a sort of breathing process.

It is these breathing cycles that Maria Thun first noticed when she observed that plants behaved differently when planted in different halves of the moon-cycle of 28 days. This is what they're about ...

There are three basic breathing cycles; two come under the aegis of the sun and one of the moon.

- **Yearly**, the Earth breathes in from the autumn to the spring equinox and out from the spring to the autumn. This is a sun-cycle.
- **Monthly**, the Earth breathes in for fourteen days of the moon's cycle and then out for the next fourteen. This is the moon-cycle.
- **Daily**, the Earth breathes in from midday to midnight, and out from midnight to midday. This is a sun-cycle.

Now, the Earth does different things when she breathes in to when she breathes out ...

When the Earth breathes in she draws energy downwards, into herself, into the soil, nourishing the soil and the roots.

When the Earth breathes out she sends energy upwards and outwards, into the leaves, flowers and fruits of the plants.

These breathing-cycles work with the rhythms of the sun – our local star – and the moon to give us the northern and southern planting times. Let's look at these in more detail.

Yearly Cycle

- from autumn equinox to the spring, over the winter, the Earth breathes in.
- from spring to the autumn equinox, over the summer, the Earth breathes out.

From midsummer to midwinter the sun travels in a lower and lower arc across the sky each day. This gives us the beautiful low, slanting light of winter. Dawn gets gradually later each morning and dusk earlier each evening, so the days get shorter and shorter, until the sun's arc sinks to its lowest point, its nadir, at midwinter. Then, at midwinter, the cycle reverses so that from midwinter to midsummer the sun rises higher and higher in the sky each day. Dawn gets earlier and dusk later, the days get longer, until the sun is at its zenith at midsummer.

As the sun's arc gets lower in the sky each day the Earth "breathes in", drawing energy down into the soil and roots. Over winter, we prepare the ground for the coming spring, putting mulches, compost and manure the beds, helping the earth to regenerate before the growing season.

When the sun's arc is rising, getting higher in the sky each day, the Earth "breathes out", drawing the energy up through the parts of the plant above the ground. This is part of what sets seeds off to germinate (along with the increasing light) and why germination is much stronger from spring to midsummer.

We see this as we watch how plants behave over the winter and summer. Winter is a time of regeneration, work going on under the surface of the soil. Summer is a time of proliferation, of flowering and pollination, making fruits and spreading seed to continue the species.

This is about light, the light of the sun. Plants, like all creatures including us, are incredibly sensitive to light. From midsummer to midwinter there is less and less light each day until at the autumn equinox (equinox means equal night) the hours of light and darkness are equal for a day. After this there is more dark than light each day up to midwinter and the shortest day. This is the winter solstice. The word solstice means "stand-still" as this is when the sun appears to stand still (rise in the same place) for three days, before it moves on, to appear to rise in a different place on the horizon each day, from the 25th December. This is the ancient sun-return time celebrated by our forebears and still by us today.

From the midwinter solstice, there is gradually more and more light each day up to the spring equinox when light and dark are again equal for one day. After this, there is more light than dark each day up to the midsummer solstice. Midsummer was a time of high celebration for our ancestors although less so for us now. The sun appears to stand still for three days, on the 25th June it moves on.

So the cycle goes around and comes around.

Seasons – The seasons happen because of the tilt in the Earth's axis. Without this there would be no seasons and they occur most prominently the further away from the equator you are, this is because the tilt becomes more pronounced. Our ancestors understood about the seasons. Winter and summer solstices and equinoxes are marked on the old stone circles.

As I said, plants are enormously affected by light. It's through light that photosynthesis happens and this is the major way for green plants to make food for themselves. Light also affects germination, plants can tell how much light there is and whether it's getting less or more. As the light decreases so does their inclination to germinate.

Some plants need the cold and frost of winter to activate their seeds into germinating. Others need a particular temperature, too little or too much and they won't germinate. Some even need fire to start them off. The warmth of the sun, or lack of it, is a vital part of what makes plants grow.

Biodynamics helps these cycles. Using the preparations in time with the star calendar helps the plants take best advantage of the light, the warmth and the seasons. As we have to change our ways to live in the new world that will come out of global warming biodynamics will help the plants, and us, to adapt successfully.

We use prep 500, horn manure, more over the winter season to help the work that goes on beneath the surface of the soil.

We use prep 501, horn silica, more over the summer season to help upper parts of the plant.

But ... we can use both preparations during both winter and summer, depending on what the plants need. Gardeners are good observers of their plants; they have to be in order to see what's needed; to add in noticing when plants need the preparations – in tune with the calendar – helps. For instance, if you have Christmas Roses in your garden they'll like a spray of 501 just before they come into flower, before midwinter. And, the taste of your Brussels sprouts for Christmas dinner will be enhanced by a spray of 501 before harvesting. Try to think of what the plant is doing and work with that, don't get rigid or stuck in a box of "500 = winter, 501 = summer", nature isn't like that.

Daily Cycle

This is a sun-cycle, similar to the annual one. The light increases from midnight to midday and decreases from midday to midnight.

- from midnight to midday the Earth is breathing out
- from midday to midnight, the Earth is breathing in

When you want to work with the roots and soil it's best done when the Earth is breathing in – when she is drawing energy down into the roots and soil, from midday to midnight on the daily cycle.

Sowing seeds, planting and transplanting are all about the roots of plants and so are best done in the afternoon when the Earth is breathing in. This refers to all plants, not just plants we grow for their roots ... all plants have roots, they are the plant's basic means of getting food and water.

Conversely, to work with leaves, flowers or fruits it's best to work when the Earth is breathing out, in the morning. At this time the Earth is drawing energy up into the parts of the plant above the ground and so prep 501 helps these parts of the plant to respond well. Foliar feeding will also have a more marked and beneficial effect if done in the morning. Basic guidelines are ...

- We use prep 500 in the afternoons.
- We use prep 501 in the mornings – with the notable exception of root veg. We use 501 on spuds, onions, carrots, parsnips, etc. in the afternoon just before harvesting to finish the crops, make them tastier and help their storage capacity, see Using 501 for details.

Monthly Cycle

This cycle covers the moon's 28 day period. For one half of her cycle the arc she travels across the sky each night gets steadily higher and higher. Then, over the other half of the month, she makes lower and lower arcs across the sky each day for the next two weeks.

Like with the sun's arcs, when the moon's arcs are rising she is breathing out, while her arcs are falling she is breathing in.

As you can see, the breathing cycles are about how the two lights of our sky, the sun (our star) and the moon, make rising or falling arcs across the sky each day.

- Rising arcs = breathing out, draw energy up through the plant.
- Falling arcs = breathing in, draw energy down through the soil.

The Monthly Cycle is about the arcs the moon makes as she travels across the sky each day, not the phases of the moon. The old almanacs called these monthly cycles of the rising and falling arcs "moon riding high" as the moon rises higher and higher in the sky each day, and "moon riding low" as she rises lower and lower during the second half of the month.

It is the rising and falling arcs across the sky that the moon makes each day which give us the sowing, planting, cultivation and harvest times each month. Our forebears knew this from observation. Using the stone circles and other astronomical constructions they made the first star calendars. Later there were the almanacs like those my dad and uncle used. Now we have star calendars like Maria Thun's.

These arcs do not always correlate with the phases of the moon although sometimes they do. The phases of the moon refer to how much of the moon is showing, new, first quarter, full, second quarter, i.e. how much the moon is eclipsed by the Earth being between the sun and the moon. This is quite different from the arc the moon travels across the sky each day.

In the rising arc the moon goes up through the constellations from the Archer through the Goat, Waterman, Fishes, Ram, Bull to the Twins. The Earth breathes out during this time so it is when we work with the parts of the plant above the soil, and with prep 501.

In the falling arc the moon sinks back down through the constellations from the Twins through the Crab, Lion, Virgin, Scales and Scorpion to the Archer again. The Earth breathes in during this time so it is when work with the parts of the plant below the soil and with the soil itself and with prep 500.

Note – the northern hemisphere's rising arcs are the southern hemisphere's falling arcs so the Northern in-breathing time is Southern out-breathing and vice versa.

We work on sowing, planting and transplanting – all work with the soil and parts of the plant below the ground – when the Earth is breathing in, pulling the energy down into the soil.

We do cultivating and harvesting – working with the part of the plant we are most interested in above the ground –when she's breathing out, sucking the energy up through the plants.

These working practices, using the sun and moon cycles, came about long after Steiner was dead (he died in 1924) from the work begun by Maria Thun in the early 1950s. Steiner left his followers saying, "I have given you the letters of the alphabet, it's up to you to make words, sentences, books from them." This is what Thun did, she took what Steiner had given and built on it with great success. Her work is extremely helpful to us and expands Steiner's work just as he suggested be done.

The most important thing the calendar helps you with is when to apply the Preparations.

Using the star calendar, you see at a glance which day is which, and which time of the month you are in, so you can sort out what you want to do and plan your gardening to take advantage of it.

When Steiner first showed his friends how to do it he didn't faze them with calendar stuff – indeed it hadn't been worked out then. Getting the preps onto the land is still the most important thing, even if the timing does get a bit off, but getting the timing right really adds oomph to the effect of the preps. It's all about working in harmony with the rhythms of the Earth, so we use the star calendar to see when to apply the preparations, particularly the spray Preparations.

Prep 500, Horn Manure, is applied on root days, in the afternoon, when the Earth is breathing in.

Prep 501, Horn Silica, is applied on leaf, flower or fruit days, in the morning, when the Earth is breathing out.
The star calendar shows us just when those days are. In the next chapters we are going to look in detail at just how you do this.

These preparations are sprayed onto the soil and the plants. Both are made in a cow's horn which is buried in the ground, over either winter or summer. They are easy to use and anyone who wished could make them – even in a small city garden.

> **Horn manure – 500** is fresh cow manure prepared in a cow's horn over the winter. It improves the soil and helps roots to come to their full potential. It is applied to the soil, but it doesn't matter if you splash the plants while applying it.
>
> **Horn silica – 501** is crushed quartz silica (crystal) prepared in a cow's horn over the summer. It helps fine tune cultivation, bringing leaves, flowers, fruits and roots to their full potential. It is applied to the plants, rather than the soil, and it must be used carefully, in time with the star calendar and on only the relevant plants, or you will get some effects you didn't want.

You need only a very small amount of either prep. For the horn manure, a piece about the length of your first thumb-joint stirred into an ordinary household-size plastic bucket half full of water will do the whole of the average town garden. For horn silica, a quarter of a teaspoon in half a bucket of water will be quite enough for most people's veg and flowers. It really is a case of less-is-more.

The preparations are not fertilisers to be sprayed onto the ground and plants in great quantities. As you'll see, you actually just flick droplets onto the soil with a large wallpaper brush or spray plants with a fine sprayer. Using the brush may make you feel a bit silly at first, especially if your neighbours see you, but you really won't care once you're munching those delicious raspberries or vegetables and enjoying the beautiful, healthy flowers.

About Cows' Horns … A cow's horn is a very special thing, and it's not the same as a bull's horn. The cow's horn is heavy, thick-walled and slender, spiralling right up to the tip. There are "rings", rather like the rings formed as a tree ages, that show

how many calves the cow has had. Bull's horns, on the other hand, are thin-walled, have no rings and are generally conical, growing without spiralling from base to tip.

People have tried putting the manure into other containers, including bull's horns as well as clay and glass pots, to see if the process still works. It doesn't. You end up with manure very like what originally went in. There's something about the cow's horn that's special – even if we don't yet know what it is – that enables the manure to turn from smelly cow pat to a fine, sweet-smelling earth-like compound. The same goes for the silica although the non-effects aren't so obvious.

I don't know why this happens and – at present – I don't think anyone else really does either, but it does work and the results on the garden are wonderful.

Note – the horns only ever come from animals after they have been slaughtered at the end of their lives. No cow is ever dehorned in biodynamics unless there is a desperate medical reason to do so. And biodynamic farmers try to use every part of the beast they are allowed to, so nothing of the cow is wasted but all is used, and with thanks.

Stirring & Application

Before you begin working with the preparations give yourself some practice at the basic techniques you'll need. It sounds really easy to stir a bucket of water but actually there's a knack to doing it without making huge waves and swamping the carpet!

The same goes for actually using the brush to apply the preps, and using the filter to get the 501 in the sprayer, and aiming the sprayer successfully so you hit only the plants you want to. So have a dress rehearsal or two before you go for the real thing.

Practice Stirring – Get a bucket of plain water and practice stirring until you get the hang of it, before doing the real thing! At first you'll likely make enormous waves and splash water all over the place! An old towel or tray to put the bucket on so you don't mess up the carpet is a good idea.

To get it right you stir in spirals from the edge of the bucket into the centre. This makes "chaos" at first and then, as you continue the motion, you stir it into a vortex of order. This stirring also gives the water a strong electrical charge – see Why Stir? for more.

And stir faster rather than slower! This may sound daft but you try it. Stirring slowly makes big slow, powerful waves that easily climb the sides of the bucket and go all over the carpet. Stirring faster makes the whole thing more controllable, the waves don't climb the bucket but stay inside, so take courage (and your stirring stick) in both hands and go for it. Stirring from the edge inwards to the centre helps this too. Stick with it! It's a knack, like riding a bike, it will come to you all-of-a-sudden.

Do not rush at the stirring but find your own rhythm and pace or you will be worn out inside a quarter of an hour. Finding your own rhythm really helps, you don't have to do it like other people. You may want to hold the stick in one hand, or like a crankshaft as I do in both hands, using the top one to steady it and the bottom one to give it circular motions. Whatever, find your own way.

Take the stick and stir vigorously in one direction, say clockwise – it doesn't matter which way. Use a spiral motion, starting at the outside and working in, until a deep vortex is formed.

When the vortex is formed as far down as you can, remove the stick for a moment, a brief breathing pause, and watch the vortex rise back up to the top again.

As the vortex reaches the top, plunge the stick back in and stir vigorously in the other direction so creating chaos again for a moment. Use a spiral motion still, starting at the outside and working in, and gradually a deep vortex of order will be formed again.

Remove the stick for a moment – brief breathing pause – then off you go again.

Repeat the vortex-chaos-vortex cycle for one hour – no less! We talk about why you do this stirring in Thoughts.

Practice Application – Unless you have vast acres of land I seriously suggest you use a wallpaper brush for flicking the prep 500, the horn manure, onto the ground. Horn manure can clog up a spray whereas, with a brush, you just don't have this problem.

If you've got a lot of land then consider getting a good-quality backpacker sprayer with an adjustable nozzle. You'll need to set it to coarse for the 500, horn manure, and fine for the 501, horn silica. A fine and narrow spray is important for the 501 so you can aim successfully and hit only the lettuces and not the tomatoes – you'll see why this is important in the prep 501 section.

And make a plan ... know your route all through the garden so you don't miss any of it. This is especially important for the 501 as you only spray some of the plants each time. But it's just as useful to be sure you've not missed any with the 500. Walk your 500-route a few times to make sure you know it, it's good to look at the garden anyway, notice how the plants are, you'll notice more and different things after you've sprayed.

I've got a "leaf-route", "flower-route" and "fruit-route" around the garden here for the 500 which pretty well ensures I don't miss anything. Roots, for 501, are different as you'll see.

It's worth being fairly competent at all these basics before you begin with the real preparations. It takes a bit of practice to learn to "flick" the brush so the drops go out over the soil – and not into your eye!

Using the paintbrush ... Dip the paintbrush into the bucket and flick it from side to side using your whole arm, giving a wide arc, showering the soil with a spray of coarse droplets

Hold the brush quite high and use a vigorous movement of the wrist; you should see the droplets go quite a way out to either side of you, like several metres.

For plant pots and in the greenhouse, as well as the indoor

plants, work much more delicately, you're not trying to make the carpet grow after all! With 500, I usually hold up the leaves of the indoor plants and aim right for soil in the pot.

Using the spray … filter the 501 preparation through a double thickness of an old pair of tights as it goes into the sprayer. You don't want to clog the nozzle with tiny bits of silica.

Find out how to adjust the nozzle so it sprays in the arc you wish. Try it out on the plants, so you know that this size works for the tomatoes while that size is best for the roses.

Find out how to pump it so it sprays evenly and practice doing this so you don't have to think about it while you're doing the actual spraying.

If you have a woodland or smallholding then you might consider getting a proper sprayer to go on the back of your quad-bike or tractor. There are several firms that can do this for you, try looking in the Smallholders Association magazine or web site.

Getting helpers – Preferably get someone, or several someones, to help you do the stirring. Stirring on your own for a whole hour when you're not used to it is very hard work. My husband and I can do it but we've been at it since the early nineteen-nineties! And anyway, it's much more fun with a friend or in a group, you can have a cup of tea, chat, get a break. Sharing the "waves" and laughing at the splashes is good too. Community biodynamics, like community composting or sharing gardens, is fun and can be a great help to everyone. Why not introduce it to your Garden Club or Allotment? When the preparation is stirred you can all share the product and give your gardens a treat.

Practising using the kit as a group is good too, you may each have ideas that help the others.

Don't get worried about exact quantities, near enough will do fine – all of the preps are good, healthy stuff, not poisons. When Steiner was asked how much to use he did exactly this, gauged the bucket size (it was a milking bucket from the farm sheds) with his eye and measured off using his thumb. He then borrowed somebody's walking stick to stir with! So if anyone starts to get precious with you about how much or what the utensils should be made of just tell them this. Steiner used what was to hand, what was available, and didn't fuss over it but got on with the job.

Chapter 3

Using Preparation 500 – Horn Manure

Timing – this stirring should be done in the afternoon or early evening, on a Root day when the Earth is breathing in: see Star Calendar chapter.

As that may still sound like complete gobbledegook it's a good idea to do your first stirring after you've read this book through once and got an idea of what I'm talking about. The star calendar chapter explains what's going on, read it a couple of times to get your head around it.

When you feel you know what you're doing have a go at your first 500 stirring. The garden will do better if you give the soil attention first – like in all organic practice, good soil makes good plants – so do the 500 first for the soil and the 501 for the plants later.

Look at your star calendar to find the right day to do the stirring – a root day, in your planting season, in the afternoon. And re-read the chapter on the star calendar in this book the day before.

Remember ... make a plan of how you are going to go round the garden spraying, especially while you're new to this.

You need ...

- Prep 500, horn manure.
- Prep 507, valerian juice; it's one of the compost preps but you use it here, with the 500 to help warm up the soil and encourage earthworms.
- A non-metallic bucket. Wood is very nice but very expensive, a plastic bucket from the household shop does perfectly well; the point is to get the preparations on the

land. Metal doesn't seem to work so well in most people's experience. You want a smooth-sided bucket, no ridges, and no ridges in the bottom either as they make the stirring very difficult. The bottom should preferably be slightly smaller diameter than the top so the sides slope upwards and outwards. This helps the stirring a lot and makes getting a vortex easier.

- A wooden stirring stick; we use a length of broom-handle about two foot long; or you can use your arm and hand.
- A small pot (plastic is fine, like a big ice-cream tub) that holds about half a litre, in which you can mash up the preparation before it goes in the bucket.
- A 6-8 inch wide soft-bristled brush – it needs to be wide and with soft bristles that will absorb the water. And it must be NEW, not one you've ever used for painting or plastering! Keep it, along with the bucket and stick, only for stirring.
- Water – half fill your bucket with rain or pond water. Not tap water with all the chlorine and stuff in it. If you have your own spring or bore-hole the water will be good with no additives. If you have to use tap water, with additives, then leave it in an open-topped container out in the sunlight for three days before you want to stir. Don't buy bottled water. The water you use should be connected with the land where you live, even if it has to be tap water. This biodynamic stuff needs a bit of planning as you can see!

Method

Warm the water up to blood temperature as follows ... Boil up about a quarter of the water in a saucepan, then pour that into the rest of the bucket. Test it for temperature by putting your elbow into the bucket – like mother used to do to test the bath water for the baby. If it's comfortable to your elbow it will be comfortable for the plants too.

Put a half a litre, a pint, into the small pot or ice-cream tub

Take the required amount of 500, horn manure – a thumb-joint's worth in half a bucket of water for the average town garden – from its storage jar and crumble it into the small pot, crush it with the stick so it begins to dissolve.

When it's fairly well mixed pour the contents of the small pot into the bucket of warm water and rinse the pot in the bucket so you don't leave any in the pot.

Decide with your friend(s) how long you are going to stir each go; Paul and I do ten minutes each then swap over, so it's ten minutes on, ten minutes off so we each get three goes at stirring in the hour.

Note the time on the clock! Begin stirring.

15 minutes before the hour is up – after ¾ of an hour stirring – put about 10 drops of prep 507 (Valerian) into the mix and continue stirring until the hour is up.

Walk around your garden – use the plan so you don't miss anywhere – flicking the prep onto the soil of all the beds and the grass of the lawn too. You put the 500 on all the soil in your garden – flower beds, veg beds, lawn, fruit trees/orchard, fruit beds, rockeries, bog garden, everywhere. It doesn't matter if you splash the plants too.

Don't save any leftovers in the bucket, it goes off after a couple of hours and is no good any more. You may find you've enough to go round twice, or that some beds can get two helpings. But don't save it, you have to make it fresh each time.

Tip ... I do the roots of dahlias and tulip bulbs – just a flick with the paintbrush – before I pot them up or plant them out for the coming season.

Chapter 4

Using Prep 501 – Horn Silica

Timing – The stirring should be done in the morning, on a Leaf, Flower or Fruit day when the Earth is breathing out– see Star Calendar chapter.

Prep 501 is, at first glance, a bit more complicated than 500 to use. For a start, it's possible to go wrong with it whereas it's really quite hard to go wrong with the 500. You need the star calendar for 501 so look at it now, you will see it tells you whether today is a Root, Leaf, Flower or Fruit day.

You may already be guessing (quite correctly) that … for a lettuce, variegated ivy or hosta you need a leaf day; for rose, cauliflower, geraniums or broccoli a flower day; for a tomato, strawberries, apples or a holly bush it's a fruit day; and for the humble spuds and carrots a root day.

Spot on! There's a bit more to it than that but let's keep it simple. You use the days devoted to the parts of the plant you particularly want to promote.

Remember, prep 501 works on the parts of the plant above the ground and it's very specific, working very closely with the star energy the moon is focusing on that day. Let's do that in layman's language.

Take that lettuce. The part you are most interested in, the part you're going to eat, is the leaves. You either want the lettuce to heart up nicely or to continue giving nice fresh leaves if it's of the cut-and-come-again variety. Either way it's the leaves you want. The same goes for hostas, grasses (ornamental or lawn), any plant you are growing for its foliage. Whereas with a rose you want the flowers; with a tomato or apple or pear you probably want the fruit; with potatoes, carrots, onions and beetroot you want the root. You use prep 501 to enhance that part of the plant.

So for our lettuce we want a Leaf day.

OK. But if we go gaily splurging about with that paintbrush we might well hit other plants beside the lettuce, plants in which we want to enhance features other than the leaves. What happens if we spray the tomatoes with 501 on a leaf day? We'll get nice leafy tomato bushes with not much fruit - not what we want at all!

Or, say we are going to do the tomatoes on a fruit day and we accidentally hit the lettuces as we're dashing about. Oops! All the lettuces promptly go to seed and bolt! Bother! I've done this and it was very annoying!

Do you see what I'm getting at? As I said, the 501 is very specific, it does precisely what you tell it to do so if you spray it on a fruit day it encourages everything it touches to fruit, to go to seed. If this isn't what you want then you have a minor disaster on your hands. Nothing that can't be fixed by re-sowing if it's veg, or waiting a bit and doing it right for perennials ... but still a darn nuisance.

So, if you spray on a fruit day you encourage everything to fruit. If you spray on a leaf day you encourage the leaves of whatever the spray touches; e.g. the lawn grows lush. If you spray 501 on a flower day it encourages the plants to flower. You have to be careful so check your star calendar to make sure you're doing the right plant on the right day.

Now the Bad News ... 501 stirring is done in the very early morning, preferably around dawn. And now, here comes the really bad bit - the ideal is that you should begin stirring half an hour before sunrise and apply the prep within two hours after sunrise ...

OK. I heard that scream! Yes, there really is such an hour as dawn, it's actually quite nice and the birdsong is fantastic. So are the sky, the colours and the clouds. And you only have to do this about 6 times a year. And just imagine those delicious veg and fruit, those gorgeous flowers with their fabulous scent that your hard work is going to produce. Yes ... I am trying to get you on side!

Even if you can't quite manage dawn you need to have got the preparation onto the plants by 09.30 at the latest. This does give you a bit of leeway as that means you have to begin stirring by 07.30. But really, the earlier you can begin the better. Around midsummer, of course, dawn is about 04.00 which is serious! But it really is worth it.

The possibility for mistakes is somewhat compounded by the early in the morning. At that hour many of us are still comatose and not thinking straight! Have a wake-up coffee before you try to think when doing a 501 to make sure you've landed back on the planet after a night's dreams so you don't make a hash of it.

This is another time when friends make all the difference! A car-load of friends arriving with croissants and fresh bread and coffee and Danish pastries and other goodies makes all the difference to how you feel. And, as a group, you're more likely to keep a check on each other against making mistakes but, even if you do, there's the friends to laugh and cry about it with.

Look at your star calendar to find the right day to do the stirring for the part of the plant you want to help. And re-read the chapter on the star calendar the day before. And book those friends to come and help!

When to do 501 ...

Leaves
Just when the leaves are coming in spring
Between pickings for leaf plants like kale and lettuce
At any time the plants look stressed
After a drought for leaf plants, including the lawn, to help good recovery

Flowers

Just as the flower buds are forming for flowering plants, including broccoli and cauliflower

At any time the plants look stressed

Again when you want a 2nd or 3rd flowering for flowers, or more spearlets of broccoli etc

Fruits

Just as or after the petals have fallen so the fruits are beginning to form for fruit plants

At any time the plants look stressed

Just before harvesting the fruit

501 for Root plants

Root plants are different! For them you spray in the afternoon, on a root day

Remember, root plants are those where you use/eat the roots... spuds, carrots, beetroot, swede, parsnip, turnip, onions, garlic, etc.

You do root plants just before they are ready to harvest. This "finishes" the plant, helping it to come to its best, it also increases its storing or standing capacity.

Planning

Make a list of the plants that need spraying, especially while you're new to this. You'll have so much to think about a list will help keep you focused. Planting in the BD groups helps enormously – see Cultivation. Try this chart as a starter.

Roots	Leaves	Flowers	Fruits
Potatoes	Spinach	Cauliflower	Beans
Carrots	Lettuce	Broccoli	Peas
Beetroots	Hostas	Roses	Tree fruit
Onions	Lungworts	Delphiniums	Soft fruit
Garlic	Grasses	Geraniums	Nut trees
Swedes	Herbs	Nasturtiums	Spindle tree
Turnips	Cotinus	Calendula	Holly
	Dogwood	Day Lilies	
	Bamboo	Lilac	

You need ...

- Prep 501, Horn silica
- Water – as you did for the 500 stirring. Remember, don't buy bottled water, it should come from the land where you live ...
- the same plastic bucket you used for prep 500 will do perfectly well for the 501
- the same wooden stirring stick will do too
- a small plastic funnel
- a sieve consisting of and a double layer of nylon stocking/tights
- a plant sprayer which gives a fine mist (it must not have been used for pesticides or herbicides) – not the brush this time!
- Friends, coffee, croissants, pastries, chocolate ...
- clock + alarm to get you up in time!

Method

Warm the water up to blood temperature as you did for the 500. Boil up about a quarter of the water in a saucepan, then pour that into the rest of the bucket. Test it for temperature by putting your elbow into the bucket – like mother used to do to test the bath water for the baby. If it's comfortable to your elbow it will be fine for the plants too.

Take a quarter teaspoon of 501 from its storage jar and sprinkle it into the water

Decide with your friend(s) how long you are going to stir each go. As for the 500, we do ten minutes then swap.

Note the time on the clock! Begin stirring.

Stir vigorously in the vortex-chaos-vortex cycle for one hour (no less) as for 500.

When the hour is up, strain the liquid through the through the funnel-and-stocking-sieve contraption into the sprayer.

Then, sprayer in hand, venture out into the dawn and spray the relevant parts of the relevant plants with the 501. You put the 501 only on the relevant plants for the day you are working – this should be in both ornamental and veg beds … rockeries, bog garden, everywhere that has plants relevant to the day, including the lawn if it's a leaf day and fruit trees/orchard as well as fruit beds if it's a fruit day. And remember it does matter – a lot – if you splash the wrong plants!

Don't save any leftovers in the bucket, like the 500 it goes off after a couple of hours and is no good any more. You may find you've enough to go round twice, or that some plants can get two helpings. But don't save it, you have to make it fresh each time.

Now … stagger back indoors and either have breakfast with friends or go back to bed.

Chapter 5

Compost Preparations

These are available ready-made from your local or national biodynamic association – you don't have to make them yourself. The compost preparations are ...

502 – Yarrow *Achillea millefolium*: Yarrow does the potassium and sulphur processes of the soil; helps replenish soil grown tired through many years of cultivation. The country name is "Venus Eyebrow" as the seed looks a bit like an eyebrow.

503 – Chamomile *Chamomilla metrecaria recutita*: Chamomile helps the living calcium processes and helps to stabilize plant nutrients; it also dampens down excessive fermentation and invigorates plant growth.

504 – Nettle *Urtica dioica*: Nettle helps iron and helps to stabilize nitrogen.

505 – Oak bark *Quercus robur*: Oak bark is rich in calcium. It helps to ward off plant diseases and fungal attacks.

506 – Dandelion *Taraxacum officianale*: Dandelion does the living silica processes; helps the natural relationships like the mycorrhiza become fully effective. The plant's country name is "Lion Tooth" from the French, dent de lion meaning tooth of the lion. Our word dandelion is a corruption of this.

507 – Valerian *Valeriana officianalis*: Valerian does phosphorous, providing a warmth blanket to the compost heap. Earthworms love it. Used with Prep 500 it draws worms into the garden and helps them reproduce well.

Making Compost – Cool Heap Method

Most books on biodynamics talk about making large heaps of compost, the hot heap method, though rarely calling it that. Hot heaps, also called windrows, are usually enormous, several feet high and many feet long. I can see some of you paling at the thought already! These are the sort of compost heaps as you get at RHS Wisley or at one of the National Trust estates or on a farm. But most of us have little wee gardens, often in cites. And we don't work as they do on big estates so we don't get masses of bulk material all at one time.

Generally for gardeners compost comes "little and often" over the whole of the year, adding weeds and kitchen waste as you have it, as the kitchen caddy fills up. This is cool heap working.

The cool heap needs the preparations just as much as the hot heap but, because it's never really finished, you use them in a different way, by using what are called compost starters. These starters are perfect for the little-and-often way of composting that works best for the average household. And your bin will get hot! Not as hot as a big heap but quite warm enough so you'll pull your hand back quickly when you put it inside the bin. They work well in ordinary plastic compost bins like the cheap ones you can get through your local council in Britain, and in home-made pallet-bins as well as the posh wooden ones.

Starter Preparations

Cow-Pat Pit is available from your local biodynamic association or you can make yourself – see Making the Preparations, it's not difficult. It is also particularly useful as an added pep-up for the soil and plants in the garden as well as working in the compost. Directions for using it this way are in the Cultivation chapter.

Mausdorfer was developed by Josephine Porter, a student of Ehrenfried Pfeiffe, who began the Josephine Porter Institute for Applied Biodynamics (JPI) in the USA. You can buy it from your local or national biodynamic association, you don't need to go the US for it. 1899-1961

Ehrenfried Pfeiffer (1899-1961) began work with Rudolf Steiner in 1920. He later developed an analytical method of using copper chloride crystallization that was used as a blood test for detecting cancer. As a result, in 1937, he was invited to work at the Hahnemann Medical College in Philadelphia and emigrated to the USA in 1940. His theory brought him an honorary degree of Doctor of Medicine from Hahnemann Medical College and Hospital in Philadelphia in 1939. He also studied chemistry and became a professor of nutrition in 1956. But he always followed biodynamics and the Josephine Porter Institute carries on the good work. It has an excellent web site and does a very good magazine "Stella Natura" for which I occasionally write an article.

Using Cow-Pat-Pit Prep & Mausdorfer

To use in the compost bin, take about an ounce of either the Cow-Pat-Pit prep or Mausdorfer and sprinkle it on the top of each layer of compost material as you add it to the bin. Because it's been mixed with cow manure and basalt it quickly works in the heap, making it brew fast and well.

Bins, Worms & Bugs for Composting

Most of us are familiar with some form of compost bin. They come in all shapes and sizes from lash-ups of pallets through posh, expensive wooden bins, bottomless dustbins or plastic ex-fruit-juice concentrate barrels, local authority-supplied plastic bins, or ones bought from your garden centre. Whatever bin you decide on make sure ...

- The compost is in contact with the soil so the worms and bugs can get into it.
- The bin gets sunlight for a good part of each day.
- The bottom is secured from rats – see Pests & Diseases.
- The compost itself is chopped up as well as you can

manage to give lots of surface area – see Colloids in the Thoughts chapter for why this is important.

Use the lawn-mower to help with chopping. Lay the compost material out on the lawn and run the mower over it. Some grass will get mixed in which helps speed things up as well. The result should be reasonably chopped material with a greater surface area than it had before. If you can afford it, get a really good shredder, one that can cope with wet material. This will improve your composting by an order of magnitude ... but good shredders cost and arm and a leg!

An average town garden may have the space to accommodate two local authority bins – they usually contain about a cubic meter or sometimes a bit more. And yes, the plastic compost bins provided in the UK at a massive discount by your local council are absolutely fine for biodynamics.

As well as the ordinary bins many people are now using wormeries compost Preparations and Bokashi. Both are excellent and can be used with the cow-pat-pit and/or Mausdorfer preparations.

Worms

Wormeries are very good, giving you solid compost and liquid feed for the plants in a fairly short period, a few months. They can be a bit fiddly and take some getting used to as the worms are as idiosyncratic as any cat or dog! Wormeries are good if you have only a small space as they deal with compost quickly and without smell or mess – once you have the knack of them.

Each time you add kitchen waste to your wormery, sprinkle a teaspoonful of cow-pat-pit or Mausdorfer onto the top of the layer. It won't harm the worms in any way ... possibly they may come out the other side even more fit and muscular than ever!

Some people say they get seriously huge worms after they've been chewing through the BD veg and the BD preps! We certainly notice how big and healthy our worms are here, how many there are in the wormery and of all generations from tiny, wee babes like a wriggling piece of cotton to enormous ones that we think came from Frank Herbert's planet Dune. My husband says he's going to set a thumper to call them! Regardless of sci-fi in-jokes, our worms are both prolific and big. Having worms of all sizes is a good sign that they're healthy and breeding well. See Cultivation for how to use the worm compost in the garden.

Bokashi

Bokashi is a Japanese system of composting using "bugs" which are applied in handfuls of a special bran supplied by whoever you got your bokashi bin from – see contacts. Within the bin it's an anaerobic process, excluding the oxygen in particular, which is different from other composting systems. We've found it very effective and much faster than the wormery – and much easier to get the hang of. The bugs are not contrary-minded as the worms can be and just seem happy to get on with their job of digesting the kitchen waste. It is more expensive in that you have to keep buying the bran for the bugs. Add a teaspoonful either cow-pat-pit or Mausdorfer with the waste material you add to the bokashi.

Bokashi is a very good way to deal with meat and fish waste. Many people worry about putting these into the heap in case they attract rats. First of all, remember that rats are omnivorous, they eat anything and everything, not just meat and fish or dairy; the ones on the farm next to where we live love the grain that falls from the straw and hay the cattle are fed, for instance. The bugs in the bokashi will deal with all the meat and fish before it ever gets to your ordinary compost bin.

See Cultivation for how to use the bokashi in the garden.

Whichever system you use – bins, wormeries, bokashi or all the lot – as you add each layer of compost to your bin, sprinkle on some of whichever starter you've chosen. They begin to work straight away, getting the compost going.

The starters will speed up the composting – provided your bin is in good condition – to give you a very good compost in six months; sometimes quicker if you chopped the material up well before putting it in the bin.

And ... you'll find you need less of the BD compost to bring the soil into good heart.

Preps in the Hot Heap Method

To use the compost preps in the way farmers and large estates do you need at least a cubic metre of "stuff" before putting the preps in – that's a heap 1m tall x 1m deep x 1m wide. Posh wooden compost bins you can buy at garden centres and in catalogues are often about this size, so are the ones you can knock up yourself from old pallets. To fill one up takes a lot of compost.

A hot heap needs to be this big so that it has enough mass to generate the super-high temperature. Hence you need a lot of material, all at once, to get it going. If/when this happens – like spring and autumn – then you can use the compost preps in the way of farmers and large-scale growers.

You Need ...

- The 6 compost preps
- An egg box
- A small amount of wet clay-soil or moist cow dung
- The trusty bucket and stirring stick
- Compost Preparations
- Gardening with the Moon & Stars
- Half a bucket of rainwater
- Watering can with a coarse rose
- A thick stick, about an inch in diameter and half the height of your compost bin/heap
- Clock

Method

It's good to be indoors, in the garden shed, or somewhere comfortable to make up the preparations into little balls ready to put into heap. Having a table and chair helps too.

Take the 502, yarrow, and open it up. Take a piece about the length of your first thumb joint. Take a piece of wet clay-soil or moist cow dung and mix it with the preparation so the two become a well-mixed ball, or egg shape. Put the yarrow-ball into the top left hand corner of the egg box – as in the pattern below

Now, take the chamomile, 503, and repeat the process. Put the chamomile-ball in the bottom left hand corner of the egg box

Now, take the oak bark, 505, and repeat the process. Put the oak-bark-ball in the top right hand corner of the egg box

Now, take the dandelion, 506, and repeat the process. Put the dandelion-ball in the bottom right hand corner of the egg box

Finally repeat the process with the nettle, 504. Put the nettle-ball in the bottom central hole of the egg box.

Now, head for the compost heap ...

You use this same pattern to put each of the balls of prep into your bin – this way you know which prep is which.

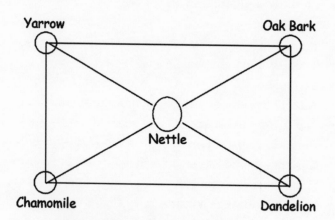

water valerian over the whole heap

Fig 3: Compost Heap Pattern

Take the thick stick that's half as deep as your bin and push it right down so it stops about half way down through the heap. Make five holes this way, as in the pattern. NB – the pattern works just as well for round bins as square.

Drop each ball of prep down the relevant hole. If necessary, give it a gentle shove with the stick to make sure it goes all the way down the hole to sit in the middle of the heap.

Now it's time to do the valerian ...

Put about thirty drops of valerian juice (prep 507) into the rainwater in the bucket and stir it vigorously clockwise and anticlockwise, making a vortex in each direction, creating the chaos as you change direction – as for preps 500 and 501 – for twenty minutes

Pour the stirred valerian into the watering can (with rose!) and water the valerian onto the contents of the bin

Put the lid back on and leave to cook! My Dad would have added, "Light the blue touch-paper and stand clear ..." but he used to set off fireworks long before there were any safety regulations!

Your compost preps won't blow anything up but they will start the wonderful process of making your heap into really excellent compost. It should all be ready for you in 6 months' time, maybe even 3-4 months depending on how well you were able to chop things up. The finer the chopping the faster the compost, it's like chewing your food, it helps digestion.

It's interesting that in 1999 the United States Department of Agriculture (USDA) researched the compost preps. They found that using the preps "could speed up the composting process, better destroy pathogens and weed seeds in the material by maintaining high temperatures longer, and change the value of the resulting compost as a fertiliser by increasing the amount of nitrate." A pretty good testimonial, don't you think?

Chapter 6

Cultivation

Biodynamic gardening is for the ordinary gardener who grows ornamental flowers just as much as for those who grow veg, but it is a bit more complicated for them than for the farmer and market gardener. We want our gardens looking good throughout the year so we have to work with that in mind as well. Biodynamics helps us but we have to understand what the preps do to use them intelligently. Just to reiterate ...

500 helps the soil and the roots
501 helps the parts of the plant above the ground
502-507 &/or Mausdorfer in making Compost
Cow-Pat-Pit prep (CPP) helps everything

Plants & Stars

This section on cultivation is about the calendar's secondary function of helping you sow, plant, cultivate and harvest the plants at the most advantageous time. All plants do best if planted and cultivated on the day which echoes the reason we are grow them.

The principles behind the star calendar are both complex and simple. The maths and astronomy (not astrology) are a bit too complex for most of us, so thank goodness for Maria Thun and others who are able to put it together so we don't have to. But the basic concepts behind why such-and-such is a root or a flower day are easy to grasp.

There has been a lot of study and research into this following Maria Thun's work after her initial study with radishes and she has continued doing subsequent studies for the past 30 years. Other people and institutions have done tests too, with the same results: if you are interested go to http://www.considera.org.

Potatoes, carrots, beetroots, onions, swedes, parsnips etc. are plants we grow for their roots. If you plant or cultivate them on a leaf, flower or fruit day they won't be so healthy, productive and tasty as they would if you worked them on a root day

You might find that the plants produced good foliage (leaf day planting) for instance and few actual spuds or carrots. However, if you cultivate them – i.e. weed, feed, thin out, prune – on a root day you'll enhance their growing and produce better spuds and carrots. If you use a non-root day they won't be as good. This affects taste, scent and storing quality as well as appearance, so cultivating your spuds on a root day makes them much tastier when you come to eat them as well as helping them to store better. Similarly, if you dig up your spuds on a root day experience shows they store much better than if you dig them up on a leaf, flower or fruit day.

To reiterate again …

Root days are when it's good to do anything connected with roots and/or the soil; sowing and cultivating plants which we grow for their roots, essentially root vegetables such as potatoes, carrots, beetroots. As all plants have roots these days can be used for anything to do with the roots of any plant, and rooting plants from cuttings too.

Leaf days are when it's good to do anything connected with leaves. They are also good for sowing and cultivating plants which we grow for their leaves such as many plants, trees & shrubs with beautiful leaves, as well as vegetables such as spinach, lettuce, cabbage, sprouts, hostas, lettuce, pulmonarias, cabbage, grasses, variegated ivy, herbs, etc. And the lawn.

Lawn mowing …

- Mowing the lawn on a *leaf* day encourages the grass to grow!
- Mowing on a *flower* or *fruit* day will encourage the grass to

go to seed!

- Mowing on a *root* day pulls the growing energy down to the roots, which also helps the grass to combat drought and flood. The leaves won't grow so fast ... so you don't have to mow so often! ... but the roots will be strengthened so the grass recovers better from droughts/floods as well as from hard wear. Mowing on a *root* day is good!

Flower days are when it's good to do anything to plants you grow for their flowers. They are also good for sowing and cultivating plants which we grow for their flowers. Such plants might be flowering perennials and annuals; flowering trees & shrubs like magnolia, wigelia, roses, fuchsias iris, clematis, mock orange; vegetables such as cauliflower, broccoli, and edible flowers like nasturtiums, calendula, day lilies.

Fruit are days when it's good to work plants grown for decorative or eating fruit such as holly, crab-apples, cotoneaster, firethorn, spindle, Chinese lanterns, apples, pears, apricots, nut trees and bushes; and soft fruit such as raspberries, currants, strawberries; vegetables such as beans, peas, tomatoes, peppers, courgettes.

Doing Your Best

All this may sound as though it's going to regiment your life and your gardening unbearably ... and make it impossible for you to do things! This just isn't so.

Biodynamics is NOT about stuffing you into a box and a straightjacket. The cycles are the way the Earth works in cahoots with the Solar System and the cosmos. By working along with her – as far as possible – we really make a huge difference to how well our plants grow. But Life happens. We have to be at work, take the kids to school, go on holiday, it rains, snows, hails, has a drought, we get sick, the car gets broke, etc. Like I said, Life happens.

The sun is not going to fall out of the sky if you can't always manage to work the garden exactly as it says in the star calendar! Mother Nature is a good mother, she knows about things going pear-shaped, about not being able to do things when you want to, she won't take it out on you!

Plants want to grow. They do their best to germinate and grow even in dreadful conditions, as you probably already know. Working with the star calendar helps them grow better. Not being able to work with the star calendar slows everything down in comparison to how you'll find it work when you are in tune with the calendar, and it won't give you the quality you would otherwise get, but the plants will still do their best to grow. And there are ways to work round it if you couldn't sow on the relevant day. So what do you do if you can't plant the spuds on a root day, when the Earth is breathing in, in the afternoon?

You do your best. For instance …

- Can you plant them on a root day when the Earth is breathing in but in the morning? That'd be two out of three right.
- Or in the afternoon, when the Earth is breathing in but it's not a root day? Still two out of three and far better than nothing; the root-day bit does matter though as Maria Thun showed.
- Or perhaps in the afternoon on a root-day but when the Earth is breathing out? That's two out of three as well.

Are you getting the idea? You do your best, you put as many of the factors together as you can and then get on with it. You can make things better later by cultivating – hoeing, weeding, feeding, etc. – the spuds on root-days, in the afternoon when the Earth is breathing in. That makes a lot of difference and can really bring the plants on. And you can give them an extra spray of 500 as another booster, and a spray of cow-pat-pit prep which will give an amazing boost to the soil itself and so to the plants. You do your best, make-do-and-mend. Good enough is always better than doing nothing.

So, life goes on even if you can't do things quite perfect. And you won't be blasted to plant-hell either! For centuries before Rudolf Steiner discovered about the preparations we grew plants and did agriculture. Yes, biodynamics makes a huge and very noticeable difference but things can still cope if you get it wrong, or when you just can't manage it quite as right as you'd like. The Earth does have several billennia of coping with mistakes and disasters and, in any case, has been growing plants for millions and billions of years, long before human beings appeared on Earth let alone discovered agriculture. So likely it will all be OK even if you can't follow the star calendar to the letter, but you will notice a difference between when you got it right, when you got it half right and when everything went completely pear-shaped, and that's fascinating learning too.

Biodynamics will help enormously with all the problems that are coming about from Climate Change. Remember, that's the same things that set the farmers and Steiner off in the first place ...

- increasing mechanisation of agriculture
- a sense that nature is becoming degraded and losing its vitality
- pollution of the environment
- signs of illness in trees and
- violent changes in the weather

Like I said before, it seems nothing is new. Now, we can see that we have had a large hand in bringing about those changes and need to completely rethink how we farm and garden – indeed, how we live. Learning to work with the star calendar helps us find out how to do this, it's about working with nature, with the

Solar System and the cosmos that gives us Life.

As with all gardening, do your best, the plants will appreciate it.

All of these cycles intimately relate the Earth with her fellows in the solar system and the cosmos, the moon, the sun and the stars. Astronomically and physically Earth is a part of this whole … the planetary and stellar bodies affect what happens on Earth. Biodynamics gives us a way of working with this natural phenomenon.

If you couldn't sow or plant on the right day then cultivate on it. Cultivation includes …

- hoeing & weeding
- raking
- pricking out
- potting on
- transplanting
- and the general fussing-over that we all do
- AND putting the preps on

Once those cauliflowers are in then, on the next flower day, in the morning and preferably in your "cultivation" season (i.e. when the earth is breathing out, when the moon's arc is rising) then get your hoe out and run it between the rows. If you can manage to do it on a flower day but the Earth is breathing in then that's still better than nowt – as me Yorkshire Mam used to say.

Hoeing is a good means of cultivating which we should all probably do more often. It moves the top earth gently, stopping crusts forming on top of the soil which stop the water getting in and encourage mould and fungal growth. It chops off the weed seedlings before they get a chance to settle in too. Remember Bob Flowerdew's advice and sharpen your hoe! As he says, a hoe is just a knife-on-a-stick … a sharp knife is at least an order of magnitude up on a blunt one. Hoeing on the day and time relevant to the plant you're growing encourages the plant to grow well.

Weeding, hand-weeding, on the relevant day (for the plant you are intending to grow, not the weed!) helps too. Weeding always helps because you are removing the competition from the plants you want. In my own, and many BD people's, experience it seems to make more of a difference, encourage the plant, when I do it on the relevant day for the plant – weed the lettuce on a leaf day.

Raking is another means of moving the soil gently, clearing debris between rows. Do it very lightly and carefully, just to stir the soil a little. Again, I try to do this on days relevant to the plant I want to encourage.

Potting on and transplanting on the relevant day is very important. Like sowing on the right day it gets the plant going much faster and stronger than doing it on just any old day. If you didn't manage to sow the seeds with all three factors – root/leaf/flower/fruit day, afternoon, earth breathing in – together then pricking out, potting on and transplanting on the right day really does make up for it. You'll see the plant "take off" … not quite like a Saturn 5 rocket but a real perk up.

Biodynamics helps plants. It gives oomph to already good organic practice. But everyone knows there are times when things just aren't possible to do as you would like. So when Life gets in the way and you cannot work according to the star calendar don't neglect the plants waiting for the "right day", just get on like a good gardener and do what's needed as well as possible.

Cultivating with Prep 501

Although using the horn silica (prep 501) is best done at dawn it's still effective if you begin a stirring at say seven or even eight o'clock and get it onto the plants by eight or nine. So you can do it more often than you might fancy if it meant getting up before dawn every time. For your veg, and for the first stirring each season, I really do recommend the pre-dawn vigil, it does make a difference to taste, storing ability, quality, colour etc. But for further applications – and I always give the plants here two or three goes of 501 over the summer – a bit later won't wreck the universe.

Winter applications of 501 are a good idea too, especially for the ornamental plants but late winter purple sprouting, late cauliflowers, early spring cabbage and those parsnips for Yule will all benefit from 501. I also give my sage an extra go after the autumn hair-cut so I have good sage for the sage-and-onion stuffing.

Up to now most BD books haven't encouraged work on ornamentals because they've all been written for vegetable growers, farmers and market gardeners. I fail to see why ornamentals should be left out. I find it really does help and encourage the winter-flowering plants, bulbs, hellebores and indoor hyacinths for a Christmas showing, or in early spring for other varieties. Christmas box and the blossom trees like forsythia and Japanese cherries benefit as well as the early spring flowers. It also means that dawn isn't nearly so early!

Don't get stuck in a box of rules with BD, think about it, work out what you want to achieve and use the preps to help you do it. Nothing is written in stone and Steiner said he gave us the letters of the alphabet … it's up to us to make words and sense out of them.

Ornamental Tips

Using the preps on the flower beds is just as helpful as it is in the veg beds. We cultivate the flower beds too, as we do the veg beds. Weed seedlings germinate in flower beds and need to be cleaned off so your flowers don't have competition for the light, air and nutrients in their bed. We need to sow, prick out, pot on and transplant just as we do with the veg.

Doing these jobs on a flower day encourages the flowers. Doing them on a leaf day encourages the leaves of ornamental grasses and other foliage plants including variegated ones. Doing them on a fruit day encourages the lovely seeds of spindles and holly, Chinese lanterns and crab apples, etc. Caring for grasses that have beautiful seed heads and things like ice plants with their lovely red-brown seed heads on fruit days helps them look gorgeous as they stand over the winter.

With the ornamental plants you use 501 on the days that encourage the various things you may want them to do. For instance Brunnera, the thing that looks like a forget-me-not with super ornamental leaves is a good example for this. In early spring it comes out of the ground in that miraculous way herbaceous perennials have and shows off its gorgeous blue flowers, then they're gone but the lovely variegated leaves stay throughout the summer, sometimes it achieves a second flush of flowers too. So, you'd like to encourage all of this.

Get the 500 out in early spring, say February but it will depend on the temperature and the weather, and give it a spray to encourage its roots to get going and perk the rest of the plant into action.

When the plant has come up again and is looking perky but not yet in flower, the buds just appearing – on the next flower day when the Earth is breathing out – you get the 501 out and give it a spray in the early morning to encourage it to flower well.

As the flowers are dying down, if you want it to seed and give you some more baby plants (mine does this pretty well!) then get the 501 out again on a fruit day when the Earth is breathing out and give it a spray to encourage it to go to seed. Don't cut the seed-heads off until the seed has fallen to let it seed where it will, or if you want to collect it then take the seed-heads in a paper bag for late summer sowing. This may look a bit untidy but think of the new plants you'll get. They do it better on their own, seeding where they will rather than saving the seed and sowing it indoors in the regular way if you don't mind hunting for seedlings.

Once the seeds have fallen, cut the dead heads off and get the 500 out to give the roots some encouragement as you've just chopped the plant about. About a week or ten days later, get the 501 out on a leaf day when the Earth is breathing out to encourage the leaves to give a good showing for the rest of the summer.

Finally, if you want another showing of flowers and the weather looks up for it, get the 501 out on a flower day and give it a go.

As I said, working with ornamentals to encourage particular traits is a bit more fiddly but can be well worth the effort.

If you enjoy competing in shows it can be invaluable; getting those dahlias to be at their peak for the show day really can be helped by judicious use of 501 ... and 500 too. For my 2004 Hampton Court garden we wanted foxgloves so I grew loads from the seedlings in the garden. However, foxgloves are not usually at their best in the first week of July, when the Show happens. First I gave the plants lots of 500 to encourage their roots to grow strong – good for the shock of transplanting for the show too, so I did it for all the plants.

We worked out that if we sprayed 501 in the afternoon on a root day when the earth was breathing in it would probably slow the flowering down. This idea came from what we knew happened with spuds and onions. It worked!

Then, just before the show itself I started to spray the foxgloves (and everything else we wanted to flower) with the 501 on a flower days in the morning. We had to be careful to get the time right – lots of biting of nails up to the armpit as we'd not done it before! – but we managed it. The foxgloves didn't flower at their usual time, the buds came later, and they looked grand for the show.

Fiddly – yes. Fun – yes! You can work with BD however you wish, it really will help you get the results you desire, you just need to think about what you want, work out what the prep can do to help that, take courage in both hands and give it a go.

As you become accustomed to working biodynamically you'll find you get the hang of knowing what's going on with the garden each day, week and season. And, knowing this, you can help that plant to do its thing better.

Using other preps in the garden

As well as using the eight original preparations, people have developed various other useful ideas out of the hints and tips Steiner left us with. Throughout the ensuing eighty-plus years people have been doing just that – Maria Thun, Ehrenfried Pfeifer, Hugh Courtney, Dr Henry Coandă, Lilly Kolisko, Sir Albert Howard, Phillip Callahan, to mention just a few. Biodynamics didn't freeze-dry at Steiner's death – nor did he wish it to! It's open to all of us expand biodynamics further. Here are some more ideas.

Cow-Pat-Pit

Cow-pat-pit is a favourite of mine. It's extremely useful because you can use it directly on the garden as well as a starter in your compost heap. It doesn't work instead of making compost but it does give the garden a big boost. You still need to make compost, the soil needs the physical humus and nourishment compost provides as well as all the goodness from the BD preps. However Cow-Pat-Pit adds extra oomph to what you're already giving by using the preps on the garden in the ordinary way.

You need (for the average town garden) ...
- 100g of cow-pat-pit
- Water
- The trusty bucket, half full of warm water.
- The trusty stirring stick
- The brush you use for the 500

- Clock

Use rain water if you can or, if it has to be tap water, then leave overnight before use to allow the fluoride and other chemicals in the tap water to evaporate as you would for the other preps.

Method

You work in the afternoon, preferably on a root day because the cow-pat-pit works on the soil and the roots of the plants. It's good to work while the Earth is breathing in but, with cow-pat-pit, you can use it at any time without causing too much confusion.

Put a half a litre of the warmed water into the small pot you use for the 500. Take the 100gm of cow-pat-pit and crumble it into the small pot, crush it with the stick so it begins to dissolve. When it's fairly well mixed pour the contents of the pot into the bucket and rinse it in the bucket-water so you don't leave any in the pot.

Stir for 20 minutes first in one direction and then the other, making a vortex, as you do for 500 and 501, then flick the mixture onto your garden with the brush you use for the 500.

Remember – You can buy cow-pat-pit, all ready for use as above, from your local or national Biodynamic association, see BD Resources page for a listing.

You can add 500 to it but this means stirring for an hour rather than the 20 minutes – your choice, it's quite OK to do 500 + cow-pat-pit all in one go.

Cow-pat-pit is used at any time to improve soil fertility. Some people spray it on three consecutive days before planting. We do three consecutive sprayings on the same afternoon; this mean an hour of stirring, broken into three portions, plus a bit longer for the spraying as you go round the same area three times. We find this works well and begin to notice the effects within a couple of days of doing the stirring. We apply it to all beds, flowers and woodland as well as veg, fruit and the lawn.

Seed Baths & Transplants

You can also use cow-pat-pit as a seed bath and spray it onto newly transplanted young plants. It activates the soil, encouraging better soil structure and breakdown of organic and inorganic substances.

Take 10gm of cow-pat-pit and stir it, as above, for 20 minutes in 1/3 of a bucket of warm water. Then immerse the seeds in this as a bath, or water it over newly transplanted seedlings. I've found the latter very helpful if the seedlings look as if they may flag.

Basalt & Minerals ...

You'll see you use basalt in making this cow-pat-pit, as you also do for tree paste. Basalt is a volcanic rock with particular properties, it's worth Googling to find out more about it.

Like many things, we don't know why tiny amounts of minerals are so necessary to plant growth and health but we know that they are.

With the "bigger is better" concepts prevalent since WWII the idea of infinitesimal amounts of something making a difference may be harder to understand, but these tiny amounts of minerals do make a big difference. Nature works with them by herself, in the wild. They are equally effective used by us in our gardening, especially in vegetable gardening as we take the plants from the soil or cut them right back in order to eat them. Consequently they don't die down and give the nourishment back to the soil as they would more often in the wild – even grazing animals don't pull up the grass, except for starving hippos who certainly do wreck their environment when they and it get out of balance! But the minerals in basalt seem to have a very strong and beneficial effect on the soil, and are extremely useful to gardeners. Combined with the cow dung, eggshells and the compost preps they make a potent mix, well worth using ... and making if you have the time, space and energy.

Worm-casts and Juice

Worm-casts – the solid compost produced by the worms – are superb soil-conditioning. I also use them as part of the seed and potting compost I make up each year. My seed/potting compost mix is ...

- 1 part worm-casts
- 1 part leaf mould
- 1 part horticultural sand
- 3-4 parts mole-hill earth.
- A sprinkle of ash from the wood-burning stove

Mole hill earth is the very best topsoil, after it has been through the mole and tipped out in his little, annoying, hillock on the lawn. I go round with a bucket and collect them, store them in the potting shed for the spring seed work.

We use the worm-casts as part of the regular soil-conditioning. Mixed with rock dust, leaf mould and BD composted cow manure it makes an excellent feed for the hard-working veg beds. The mix is put on as a top dressing and gently worked into the topsoil in late winter. My soil conditioning mix is ...

- 100gms rock dust (this is basalt)
- 1 bucket leaf mould
- ½ bucket composted cow manure
- 1 bucket worm-casts

Horse manure will do but remember the horse doesn't have the 4 stomach process of the cow. If you use chicken manure then use only ¼ bucket as it's so strong – and it MUST be well composted or it will scorch the ground and plants.

As well as worm-casts the worms give you a regular supply of juice. Dilute this 1/10, one part worm-juice to ten parts water, for an excellent feed.

Bokashi and Juice

The solid matter from the bokashi process is processed differently to worm-casts. The first part of the bokashi process, in the bin, is anaerobic but the second part is aerobic.

When your bokashi bin is full, set it aside for two weeks to mature, for the bugs to do their work in the anaerobic conditions. Then, after two weeks your bokashi will be ready for the second part of the process. You can either put the solid matter into your compost bin and work it through your normal compost cycle or dig it directly into the ground.

It makes an excellent addition to the compost, setting off the activity again and heating things up. The resulting compost benefits greatly from the addition of bokashi. However, I find it's really beneficial to dig it straight into the ground, we do that a lot each spring here.

To dig it into the ground you dig a trench, a spit deep – that's the depth of your spade, usually about a foot deep. Put the bokashi into the trench in an even layer along the bottom and backfill with the soil. Leave for two weeks before sowing/planting; I also water with bokashi juice three times during this holding time. The resulting bed is very well fed and consequently crops very well.

Like the wormery, bokashi also produces a juice that can be diluted and watered onto the plants and soil and, again, you dilute this 1/10 for a good feed.

Remember – both the worm-casts and the bokashi have also had cow-pat-pit or Mausdorfer added as you made them, so both are providing the BD compost preps to the soil as well as their own goodness.

Propagating

Propagating, taking cuttings, splitting and dividing perennial plants is part of life for a gardener. With non-hardy and half-hardy herbaceous plants it's often better to propagate them this way than trying to grow from seed. As well as giving us lots more plants it is fascinating to watch things take root and grow. It's fun to swap plants with other gardeners too, you get new and rare varieties, learn more about plants and there's the social angle too.

Often growing from cuttings is the best way to propagate with things – like tender lavenders and salvias for instance. As flowering plants get old they need renewing, cuttings are an excellent way of doing this and, again, biodynamics helps.

For timing, there are two ways of thinking on this front: cuttings need roots as soon as possible so they become self-sufficient – to take them on a root day. Or you can take cuttings on the relevant day for what you want them to do encourages that part of the plant – flowers on flower days etc.

There is logic in both arguments. Whichever you choose, it is best to take them in your planting season, when the arcs of the moon are falling, as this is when plants take root most easily. Taking them in the afternoon helps this process too.

My preference is to take cuttings on root days, then cultivate them, including transplanting and final planting, on the relevant plant day. The logic is that firstly I'm encouraging the roots, the mainstay of the plants and helping them establish as quickly as possible. Then, by potting on and transplanting on the relevant day, I encourage the plant to do what I would like it to – flower well, produce beautiful foliage, have glorious seed-heads. And I use preps 500 and 501 as part of the process too.

500 work

I prepare the potting compost with 500 before I start – this is best done a few days before you're going to pot up the cuttings. I make my own potting compost – see above for mix – from our own compost-bins, leaf mould and mole-hill earth that I collect whenever I see a molehill. Moles produce superb soil in their little hills, even better than soil that's had nettles growing in it although that is wonderful too. I also add sand that is very high in silica which I have to buy in. As we have a wood-burning stove the ash from that gets composted and used on the garden and in the potting composts too.

I dip the ends of the cuttings in a small amount of freshly stirred 500 as I'm potting up. This means adding another hour to the work, if you can manage it, to stir up the 500. You only need a little bit so I use a tiny amount of 500 in a Pyrex bowl and stir with a wooden whisk – all kept for gardening purposes of course. As it's a root day, any left-overs go to the indoor plants pots. NB – don't forget your indoor and conservatory plants when you do ordinary stirrings as well!

When potting on and transplanting, I use 500-prepped compost again (my own make, as above) and do the deed on the day relevant to what I want the plant to do – flower, foliage, fruit.

I prep the ground where the plant is finally going to be with 500 too, before the final planting on the relevant day for what I'd like the plant to do – flowers, foliage, fruit.

501 work

I use 501 after the plant is in its final position.

For foliage, I use the 501 on a leaf day when the foliage is starting to come through strongly. For instance, with grasses, lungworts or hostas, I would do it first when the new spring growth was coming up strongly. Then I'd do another spraying when foliage is fully up.

For flowers, I use the 501 on a flower day when the first buds are showing, not until. I give second and even third doses during the flowering period as I find this helps maintain colour and scent, as well as extending the flowering period.

For fruits, I use the 501 on a fruit day when the flowers are just falling, petals dropped and the fruiting process about to begin. I have several roses that do beautiful hips so I use this with them after working with their flowers. I also do it with my spindle tree as both flowers and fruits are spectacular on this. The process also works well with nut trees.

When I take hardwood and softwood cuttings – which may be as a part of pruning – the processes are the same.

As always in gardening (and biodynamics) think what you want to do, what you're trying to achieve and work towards that. If this means adapting what you know, what you've learned and read, then do it. A garden is a process ... never a finished thing, it's always alive, growing and changing. So is biodynamics.

Pruning

Pruning helps things grow – even lawn-mowing is pruning! It's best done when the energy is going to the roots rather than when it's speeding upwards into the stems ... that you are just about to cut! If you do pruning on root days, you'll find the sap is less conspicuous on these days ... because the energy is being drawn downwards, rather than up into the plant, so you cause less damage and are less likely to set off disease in an open wound on the plant. The old almanacs used to encourage this, pruning when it was moon riding low, i.e. in the falling arc.

With the BD calendar we are able to refine this idea further and work more closely in tune with nature. So, I usually do pruning on the day for the plant as follows ...

Apple tree – you want the apple to fruit, so ... you choose a fruit day, when the Earth is breathing in, in a falling arc for your planting time, and work in the afternoon. Does this make sense for you? It certainly seems to for the plants.

Using a fruit day for the apple, or a flower day for roses, or a leaf day for bamboo, means I work with what I would like the plant to do best. Choosing a time when the Earth is breathing in means the sap is being pulled down into the roots so there is less likelihood of damage and it encourages the roots to help heal the cuts made by the pruning. Working in the afternoon amplifies the breathing in effects.

500 work

After pruning, it helps to give an application of 500, on a root day in your planting season, falling moon arc, moon riding low.

As well as enhancing the shape of the tree pruning encourages the plant to make new growth and improves its vigour. If you give the soil around its roots a dose of horn manure you strengthen them so they support new growth more easily, so the tree does better.

This kind of dosing with 500 can be done throughout the year with the various prunings and cuttings-back we have to do on flowering plants and on fruit trees too.

501 work

Later, when the tree is sprouting again in spring, you can work serially – as I do with the Brunnera for instance – with 501.

First encourage the leaves to grow by spraying with 501 just as the leaf-buds are forming

Then, as the flower buds come, give them a 501 spray too

And finally as the flowers drop do the first 501 spray for the apple fruits you want

Do a second 501 as the first fruits form

Then a third after the first "drop" to encourage the good fruits

And a last 501 before you harvest

This is more complex working with the preps but well worth it once you get used to gardening with the moon and stars.

Chapter 7

Rotation & Garden Planning

In planning the planting of the veg garden each year I try to keep things that will require the same preps together.

Crop Rotation?

There are two arguments here: one is in favour of crop rotation and the other is in favour of "forest gardening". I use both in the garden here. Forest gardening is very good and works well with biodynamics, if you're interested look it up on the internet, there are many good books and courses you can go on to find out more. Using 501 in the forest garden needs to be very delicately done!

Crop rotation is a technique used in vegetable gardening and farming. The four-field system was introduced to Britain in the eighteenth century as a way of minimising pests and encouraging the soil. It follows on from the ancient strip-field farming is still visible in places, for instance on the cliffs above Boscastle in North Cornwall where there is still an ancient field system being worked, called The Stitches. The National Trust, who own it, encourage their tenants to continue farming in the old rotation system on these mediaeval strip fields.

The usual rotation is a four year one, hence the four-field system – brassicas or heavy feeders, followed by legumes that fix nitrogen, followed by roots that are lighter feeders, and finally a year of fallow. This succession can be varied and more often gardeners use a potato-brassica-legumes-onions rotation. The point is not to grow the same plant-family in the same bed year after year because this encourages the pests and diseases of that family to proliferate, for instance club root in cabbages. Growing a different family of plant in the next succession also encourages it to take up the goodness left by the previous one.

Plant Groups

I use the groups Root, Leaf, Flower and Fruit for planning the vegetable beds each year. It combines biodynamics with rotation and makes it much easier to work with the preparations. Our first Hampton Court show garden, built in 2004 to celebrate the 80th anniversary of Steiner's first lectures on biodynamics, was done in this style. The four terraces on the left of the garden are the four groups. Starting with roots at the bottom, the next terrace up was for leaf plants, then flower plants and finally fruits. We had great fun with the flower terrace as many people didn't realise how many flowers are edible so we had calendula, hardy geranium, day lilies, nasturtiums and rocket in flower as well as cauliflowers and broccoli plants. I think the Biodynamic Garden at Garden Organic follows similar principles.

For the show garden we also grew some vegetables on to seed which people found quite stunning. If you haven't seen a leek go to seed, or a parsnip, lettuce or a beetroot, then you don't know just how beautiful they are. I always let a few veg go to seed in the garden here, both to save the seed for the next year and for the beauty of the plants themselves. The bees, butterflies, insects and birds love it too. We really do have to climb out of the "tidy" box inherited from Victorian and early twentieth century gardeners or we miss out on how attractive they are, as well as not saving our own seed or feeding the wildlife.

So, the rotation system follows the days as shown in the star calendar and covers the plant groups as follows ...

Root	Leaf	Flower	Fruit
Potatoes	Cabbages	Cauliflower	Beans
Carrots	Lettuces	Broccoli	Peas
Beetroot	Spinach	Calabrese	Tomatoes
Onions	Brussels sprouts	Purple Sprouting	Peppers

Garlic	Leeks	Romanesco	Sweetcorn
Radishes	Chard	Geraniums	Aubergine
Parsnips, Swedes	Many Herbs	Nasturtiums	Tree fruit
Turnips	Lettuces	Calendula	Soft fruit
Horseradish	Salad leaves	Day Lilies	Nut trees
		Lavender	Some herbs

This makes it much easier when it comes to spraying 501 as all the plants who need to be sprayed on root days are together, ditto leaves, flowers and fruit. The chance of accidentally spraying the lettuce on a fruit day is considerably lessened if they are just not in the same bed as the peas. As I said, if you get that one wrong you can really mess up, make your lettuces bolt, get the spuds producing tons of foliage or flowers instead of potatoes, slow down the tomatoes. Having each type of plant together that needs the same BD treatment means you only go round those particular veg beds with the 501 each time.

As you can see, there is some mix-up of the usual rotation of the usual kind, through the plant families. Brassicas, for instance, are grown either for leaves, flowers or roots so appear in three of the columns but they take up a lot of space as well as needing protection from both slugs and butterfly caterpillars so I grow them in separate beds from other plants so they can be covered, nematoded and provided with slug pubs. It can all be worked out with a bit of planning. These plantings can be moved around so I don't grow cabbages in the same bed year on year.

Of course, you still have to go round the ornamental flower beds which are unlikely to be designed on the same lines ... although you could lay them out to follow the leaf-flower-fruit idea. In some ways we do, e.g. a grass bed, but I like to have something different in there as well, a focal point or contrast, so it's unlikely to work out as easily as it can for the veg plot.

The veg garden here at Archenland is potager in style. Flowers and companion planting help to keep the balance and encourage insect and bird predators to deal with most of our pests. It also gives a visual feast for the eye and soul as well as the stomach.

Thinking this way is an art as well as a science. Chefs at posh restaurants use colour and shape in designing meals all the time, of course. We do it here in the garden too – while still maintaining the plant groupings.

Roots – bright green, feathery carrot tops beside the strong, greyish upright onions and red-veined leaves of beetroot is a lovely sight; bright, delicately cut parsnip leaves beside the thicker, paler leaves of the Swedes gives a real textural contrast show in the colour green

Leaves – leeks are stately and architectural beside the wonderful purple and green of the cabbages; rainbow chard is just spectacular; the subtle greys and greens and purples of chard and their curly leaves are lovely to look at as well as eat

Flowers – purple sprouting mixed yellow and orange calendula; geraniums and day lilies edging the cauliflower; nasturtiums and broccoli; I also put dahlias in the veg garden too, their spectacular flowers are good for cutting and they look fantastic.

Fruits – runner beans flowering alongside the corn tassels is a lovely sight; the greenhouse with the purple aubergines hanging on the vine alongside the red tomatoes looks quite spectacular

It's fun to work with colour in the veg garden.

A bit of planning – a good way to spend the dark winter evenings beside the wood-burner with the seed catalogues – will show you how to plan the planting to work biodynamically, colourfully and to help the plants. It takes the way veg feed us to the level of beauty as well as taste, nourishment and sustenance.

Chapter 8

Soil, Manure & Compost

Soil

Soil is the most important thing for all organic gardeners, including those who also work biodynamically. Good soil makes good plants, healthy, better able to resist pests and diseases. The plants are stronger in all ways, in colour, scent and flavour, than those that have to grow in tired, over-used, over-chemicalised ground. And, in good healthy soil, the pest species are far more likely to be in balance and so not so likely to cause trouble.

For instance, like everyone we have slugs here but we grow hostas, lettuces, all the best slug-bait plants, usually without having them shredded. Ditto snails, aphids etc. and I've seen vine weevils about but I don't lose everything – well, anything for many years! – to them. Our beans don't seem to get blackfly – except the year I stupidly planted them next to the elder tree! Our spuds have only once suffered the blight and that was in the ghastly flood-summer of 2007. Good soil means the whole ecosystem is in balance.

Good soil also encourages the birds. We have an ample supply of bluetits, for instance who, along with a nice complement of ladybird larvae, munch away at the greenfly. The blackbirds keep the lawns free of leatherjackets. And there are lots of bees and butterflies to do the pollination for us ... they exchange their services to us for lots to eat and good habitat for themselves in our hedges.

Everything gets the biodynamic treatment here, the semi-wild field hedges, the lawns, the shrubbery and woodland, the ornamental flowerbeds, the pond and its flora, as well as the veg beds. The garden is a wholeness, it's a place of itself, it all gets the treatment and each part of it gives and exchanges with all the other parts. And it all has good soil.

Prep 500 and the compost preps are a vital part of this. Using them brigs the soil, the land, into hood heart as it's called in gardening and farming circles. I like that phrase – in good heart. It's about working in time and in tune with the Earth. We don't work against her, try to force her into doing things our way but change our own ways and outlooks so that we work with her. She does have enormously more experience in keeping a planet in good heart than we humans, after all.

The biodynamic preps somehow make links and threads with the mycorrhiza that people are now coming to realise are so vital to good soil and good plants. Mycorrhiza fungi colonize the plant's living root system which means that they can extend the plant's root system up to 1000 per cent further into the soil. This special relationship between trees/plants and mycorrhiza has evolved over tens of millions of years. There are two types and they are found on roughly 99 per cent of plant life; one is visible and lives on top of soil and on roots, the other is microscopic, living inside of roots. In poor, urban or industrially farmed environments where the soil is compacted, and where any chemicals, insecticide, fungicide or fertilizer are used, the relationship between mycorrhiza and the plant roots cannot exist.

On the other hand, research has shown that using the biodynamic preparations somehow helps the relationship between mycorrhiza and plant roots.

In exchange for sugars and simple carbohydrates, the fungi pass on minerals and absorb moisture to aid in plant growth and survival. Mycorrhiza are made from a root-like structure and have a network called mycelium that is outside of the tree roots and goes into the soil. Mycelium absorbs nutrients and gives them back to the plant. The result is an increase in surface area for root absorption. The fungi also help with erosion control in soil. They form a glue that prevents particles from breaking apart and down. Note that point about the increase in surface area for absorption, we talk about this later in Thoughts, under Colloids.

However they do it, the preparations really help the soil, the foundation for the plants. And ... if we could just add one inch of good topsoil all over the surface of the Earth that would absorb all the carbon we have thoughtlessly created in the last hundred years of massive economic expansion. That's a wonderful thought ... and it tells us just how clever the soil is, and the Earth.

Manure

Manure is amazing stuff. If we or any animals keep it inside our bodies the result is constipation and we can die of it because it poisons us. But if we let it out, let go of it, and then compost it properly it becomes the most wonderful food for the plants that feed us, body and soul.

The Earth has arranged herself so that she uses everything. She is a closed system environment where everything is recycled, or was until we started messing with it too much. There is some external input in the form of sunlight; there's also cosmic dust, meteorites, etc. but those are very small. The Earth has always been working, as Steiner advised us to do back in 1924, as a self-sufficient and self-sustaining system. So manure is part of the whole; it's what the Earth has designed into her system. We need to learn this, get over our prejudices if we have them and use it too. We can help by composting it, this is much faster than just letting it work its way back into the soil as it will. If we add the biodynamic preps as well then we're upping our usefulness by an order of magnitude.

Manure was difficult when we lived in London. We could get horse manure but cows were rarer than hen's teeth and getting cow manure was like asking for platinum! We eventually found a source, a wonderful woman who called her company "Lady Muck" and were able to get bags of her stuff by mail order. Unfortunately she gave up due to family circumstances. Luckily, we found other sources, including biodynamic farmers, when we moved out to Hereford.

You may well find yourself in a similar situation. Do have a hunt around for cow manure. It's amazing stuff. Unfortunately most of it is still not organic and so full of steroids, immunizations, TB testing stuff, worming drenches, pneumonia injections, etc. and all the pesticides and fertilisers industrial farmers use on their land and the crops that become cattle fodder. You might like to remember that these all also go into the milk and meat you eat too. They may well be part of the reason things like MRSA, C-Diff and E-coli are so resistant to antibiotics and so lethal to us now. Worth a thought.

Good composting, especially hot-heap composting, will deal with most of these things but you must to do it really thoroughly. Hot composting can be difficult for the small-scale gardener because it requires a large amount of mass to build up the heat. However, it's possible with manure because you are likely to get the stuff delivered all in one go and can build your heap straight away. And manure itself is very good at getting up to some hairy temperatures. Add the BD preps to it, then leave it to cook for a good six months. The heat – a good hot heap will actually burn you if you put your hand in it – and the preps will sort out the drugs and poisons in the manure to leave you with a good product to use on your garden. If you go this way then getting the manure in and starting the process, getting the preps in, by June would give you usable manure the following February or March. Gardening always needs planning and project management.

You should compost horse manure in a similar way. Get the stuff by midsummer and compost it over the winter for use the following spring, or begin it in late winter for use as a mulch the following autumn. You'll need the time so that you can put the BD preps through it. You may well get reasonable stuff in three to four months but six months makes it pretty safe from any residue left by medicines and chemicals the animals have had.

Horses, get all sorts of medicines, wormings, drenchings, and their food may well have been produced chemically, even be from GM crops, so it isn't necessarily any safer than industrially farmed cow manure.

All manure needs to be composted. It's not good or safe to put it straight onto your land – although many modern, industrial farmers do just this. For one thing raw manure, especially chicken manure, is very abrasive, its chemical quality will "burn" the soil, causing damage when spread straight onto the land. It also leaches nitrogen and other elements from the land in order to break down thoroughly. One of the reasons compost bins have no bottom but are directly in contact with the soil is so that the compost can get the stuff it needs to process – like nitrogen – from the soil.

The composting process changes manure, weeds, kitchen waste, back into soil again, from which it came, into the plants, the animals, into you, and then gets put back through the waste products, including manure. Whatever manure you are able to get, put the preps in and compost it yourself for six months.

Cow Manure

This is special. Cows (and all ruminants) have four stomachs so the food is processed very differently from the rest of the animal kingdom which only has the one stomach. The end result has been digested in four different ways, four times, and is of particularly high quality. Organic, or biodynamic, cow manure is the best thing … if you can get it.

Other Ruminants

Goats, sheep and deer also have four stomachs but it can be hard to get their manure – though some people do over-winter their goats and sheep in deep litter so the manure is more readily available. Their dung is still good if you have it or can get it, and if you compost it well, with the preps, before using it on your garden. People living out on the moors or on deer farms may be able to get and use deer manure, the same goes ... compost it with the preps.

Horse Manure

The horse has only one stomach but does produce good manure. Roses love it, as has been known for ages. It hasn't been digested in the same way as cow manure, nor will it have been produced from the same sort of food. Horses and cows eat similar food but not all the same; for instance it's quite unusual to give cows oats but horses love them. The components of manufactured horse and cattle food are quite a lot different. In towns and cities it's often quite easy to get horse manure as there are usually livery stables around the town because riding is very popular. It's well worth finding your nearest stable and seeing what the arrangements there are for collection/delivery.

You need to remember that horses are given lots of chemicals too, medicines and other things. Their food is unlikely to be organic either and may even be GM. composting will deal with it.

Chicken Manure

All bird manure is "fierce" and can burn the land if not well composted. Birds are totally different creatures than animals, they eat different stuff and digest differently and, although they produce manure, it's not like animal manure. You've probably already noticed how it looks and smells quite different. Over the past 80 years biodynamic research has shown that it has somewhat different effects on soil and plants to using animal manure. Ideally, we try to use some of all types of manure – as nature does in that both animals and birds live on the Earth and defecate, so giving it their dung.

Bird digestion is very different from that of animals. Their stomach is an amazing affair consisting of two chambers. The proventriculus is the first chamber. It secretes acid for breaking down food, and is best developed in birds that swallow entire fish and other animals containing bones which must be digested. Bird stomach-acid can have a pH as low as 0.2. The stomach-chamber of birds like the shrike which eats small animals, especially rodents and songbirds, can digest an entire mouse in only three hours!

The bird stomach's second chamber is known as the gizzard whose main function is to grind and digest tough food. Birds pick up grit and small rocks as they peck seeds from the ground and this accumulates in the gizzard which grinds the particles against seeds, smashing them. Turkey gizzards can actually pulverize English walnuts and steel needles! Grebes swallow their own feathers, which accumulate in the region between the gizzard and the intestine following it. This feather-clogged zone then serves as a filter for sharp fish bones that somehow make it past the stomach.

Once food leaves the gizzard its voyage through the intestines is fairly similar to that taken by food in our own intestines; nutrients are absorbed into the body, and waste is eventually excreted.

Bird manure is useful. There are several companies who produce it all nicely bagged up as pelleted organic chicken manure that you can buy at your garden centre, or by mail order, or over the internet. However, the pelleted stuff is near impossible to re-compost using the BD preps as it's all in little hard, dry lumps that shut out anything else getting into them. Added to your general compost heap they can be composted but will take a long time.

You may be able to get a load of chicken manure straight from somebody who keeps chickens, when they're cleaning out their hen-house, or even be lucky enough to keep a couple of hens of your own as many people are doing now

Find a small-scale, organic producer who will let you have some chicken manure and you're onto a winner. Personally, I just wouldn't ever go near one the huge battery farms. The things they do to the chickens, de-beaking, crowding so the hens peck each other to death, standing always on slats with nowhere to roost or perch, the stuff they feed them on, the pain and misery the birds suffer, it's all too much for me. I won't support anything such farmers do, nor use their manure.

However, you can compost it as you would industrial cow manure, to remove the drugs. For me – and I don't like industrial milk farming either – the battery houses just go right outside the pale. However, if you can cope with this then compost the chicken manure as for the cow and horse manure, with the preps, for a good six months before you put it on the land.

Pets

Cats, dogs, rabbits, hamsters, guinea pigs, mice, rats – are all lovely companions and many of us have them. They too produce manure that can be composted and used, although in far smaller quantities than cows and horses.

Handling faeces, pets, farm animals, horses, human, should always be done using rubber gloves and you should wash thoroughly afterwards as well. There are, unfortunately, nasty diseases that are sometimes transmitted from pets to humans and you don't want this. Getting into a good hygiene routine when dealing with cleaning their litter is good practice anyway so you might as well compost the waste and use it in the garden rather than adding it to land-fill.

You'll know what your own pets have been eating, you'll have fed it to them or seen the remains if they catch. And it's probably all good quality stuff because you love them and want them to do well. My cats are outdoor cats as we live in the country but I always have a litter tray for them through the winter and a bin to compost it in. The kitty-compost gets done for a good six months but, as it comes little and often, like the kitchen waste, I use cow-pat-pit and/or Mausdorfer to work the magic. Every time I clean the litter I add it to the cat-compost bin along with a sprinkle of the starter. This takes the smell away too and sets the stuff of composting straight away.

Bokashi can do cat and dog manure too. If you walk your dog and use a doggy-bag bring it home and compost it rather than throwing it in a bin to go to landfill.

Human manure

I don't use this but some people do. It has even more dangers for us than our pets because, of course, we can very readily catch diseases from each other because we're of the same species. You can get it, chemically treated so that it should be free from all infections and diseases. However, this process kills off everything, the good bugs as well as the bad, so it's really only useful as a soil improver to give bulk and moisture retention.

Compost toilets are getting better known now and you may be in a position to consider this. If so, like everything else, put the preps through it and compost it for a good six months. As with animals, the less antibiotics and other medications you need to use the less will need to be processed out of the compost. Again, you put a sprinkle of Mausdorfer or cow-pat-pit down with the sawdust each time you go. I would give this a year before using it and I'd also tump it up – make a heap, a special human-manure heap – and put the compost preps in as well. Belt and braces stuff, because I know I can catch all sorts of diseases from human waste and I don't want to!

If possible, the very best way to deal with human waste is to use the willow-reed-beds system rather than using it as compost on one's garden. Trees are superb at dealing with all the stuff that comes out of us, including heavy metals from tooth-filling residue, canned food, and other weird things people eat. Trees are able to transmute the stuff and give it back into the soil, then give us clean, fresh water at the end of the process. I wish all the local authority sewage systems would go this way – maybe they will, in time.

Home-made Compost

Homemade compost is good – always provided you made the heap properly in the first place. This really is worth the effort to learn. Badly made heaps produce nothing but disgusting smelly sludge or dry rubbish that is no good to man nor beast. In Britain, the Garden Organic organisation (was HDRA) has begun doing training for Master Composters. These are volunteers who have learned various methods of composting and are willing to help others to learn too, free, in schools, gardening clubs, one-to-one, groups, village and town halls, all sorts of places. The organisation also does excellent leaflets and books that are easy to read and follow, and usually not expensive. And there are fact-sheets to help you on their web site.

Get competent at making compost then add the BD preps/starters for organics with oomph! You'll find you need less BD compost than the ordinary organic stuff, it goes further and helps the plants do better.

It's important that your heap is well made and not just thrown together by guess and by god, with a hope it will work OK. Your preps won't stand much chance if your heap isn't working; if it's full of lawn mowings rotting into black sludge; or old tree branches; too much "brown" or too much "green"; too dry; too wet, etc.

If you don't already know how to make compost go and find yourself a good little book on how to, read it and follow the instructions. Your local authority will probably have one, nice and simple with lots of pictures and diagrams, or ask at the Town Hall or the Library. The latter may well have some good, modern stuff on composting that doesn't make you feel you need to turn yourself into an ancient Victorian gardener. Keep an eye out for composting events and workshops too – look for "Love Food, Hate Waste" on the web. The people doing these events – master composters – will know just how to help you, will be down-to-earth gardeners like yourself, and it won't cost the earth! The Garden Organic site in the UK is good for compost workshops and runs the Master Composter scheme.

Quick guide to making compost

Composting is like the digestive process, if the stuff you put in your heap is chopped up (like chewing your food) then it's able to be digested, composted, more quickly. This is partly because there's more surface area for the bugs to get their teeth into – see colloids again in the Thoughts chapter. Large lumps of stuff are hard to digest both for us and the compost heap, less surface area.

At Archenland we chop up the stalks and old leaves, cores, all the discard stuff from cooking, at the time we're making the meal. It only takes a moment or two and then it's already chopped when it goes into the caddy, the caddy full of chopped waste goes into the compost bin and it's all done.

Tip – for tough cabbage stalks get a lump hammer and bash them! They take forever to compost if not broken down; crushing them with the hammer makes it possible for the bugs to get into the stalks and break them down really quickly. The same goes for all fruit stones and nut shells which, otherwise, will stay whole for years in your heap.

With weeds it's a bit different. If there's only a few it's not hard to chop them up by hand with the secateurs, shears and/or loppers but, when there's a lot, I find the easiest way is to spread out the pile of weeds out on the lawn and run the mower over it. If you keep the bag on then you can just tip the contents of the bag straight into the bin each time it gets full. It's a fairly quick and relatively painless way of chopping up large amounts of weeds. There's a bit of a mess on the lawn but a couple of passes with the mower after the weeds are done soon sorts that out. The addition of a bit of grass along with the weeds helps accelerate the mix.

Your compost will go much quicker, hotter and more evenly if the stuff is well chopped and mixed as you put it in. Make sure you have your "greens" and "browns" balanced, that the heap isn't too dry nor too wet. If you find you have a lot of soft green stuff to go in then get some chopped straw, crumpled newspaper, cardboard, shredded twigs or some such to go in with it. Never add too much of any one thing at a time. Compost bins are omnivores – like human beings – they eat anything and every-thing but (like humans again) they enjoy variety and no big chokey lumps.

We use rock dust (crushed basalt) and calcified seaweed to get the compost up to optimum quality. A little sprinkle along with the starter really improves it as our veg garden testifies.

Local Authority Compost

Many local authorities in Britain collect the green waste from households and process it in large, hot heaps to produce compost that people can buy back, very cheaply, to put on the garden. Some of this has been processed sufficiently to even qualify for use on Soil Association certified organic systems.

I use it, and find it very helpful, on the flower beds and as part of my seed and potting-on compost mixes. Of course, it's not as good as our own compost but I increase its value to the plants by re-composting it again, putting in the biodynamic preps. This certainly does make a difference. For instance, when it arrives from the council there are pretty well no worms in it ... after BD composting with us it's full of worms and beneficial bugs.

The biodynamically re-composted green waste is definitely worth the effort and I recommend you give it a go ... nobody ever has enough compost of their own!

Chapter 9

Pests & Diseases

Pests and diseases, the little darlings, are major bug-bears of gardeners. Slugs, snails and rabbits that munch cheerfully through your salads before you get the chance; aphids that cause havoc with the roses and honeysuckle; blackfly murdering your beans; leatherjackets wrecking the lawn; mice eating the pea seeds and all the other critters that want your plants. Then there are all the diseases the plants can get. Gardening can be a nightmare!

Biodynamics does not eradicate pests, this is quite contrary to its ethos, but it does help you put the garden into balance with itself, and its surroundings which really makes a huge difference to how pests and diseases work (or don't!) in your garden.

Pests and weeds come when things are out of balance, when you have row upon row of lettuces just asking for slugs to come and make a feast, with nothing to get in their way. The darn lettuces seem to actually be singing siren songs to the slugs! And in a sense they are. Nature abhors a vacuum. And she abhors gluts too. This doesn't mean you must grow fewer lettuces but it does mean it's worth doing what you can to help maintain the balance. Gardens are not natural places, they are made by human beings – as is most of our countryside in the populated world. Therefore we are a part of the system we have made and need to work with it to help it work well. Gardening with the moon and stars helps us do just that.

The spray preparations – the 500 horn manure and the 501 horn silica – help the soil and the plants reach their optimum potential. This happens, even if we don't really know why. We don't know why electricity works, but we're quite content to trust the light switch will work whenever we want, we may even get cross when it doesn't. With a little practice we can become equally blasé about biodynamics and with equal justification. We know how to make electricity work even if we don't know why it does it. We can learn how to make biodynamics work as we have learned how to make electricity work and, again, without needing to know why it does it. And it does work. A part of its work is to help the garden grow into balance with itself, and stay in balance, so the pests and diseases don't trouble us. It's worked well for me since 1990.

So ... the first thing to do, to deal with pests and diseases, is to get your garden working well, in balance, by using the spray and compost preparations.

Pests

Pests are just about anything the gardener has a problem with, animals, insects, birds, butterflies, other people, children ... Usually, it is anything that wants to eat or otherwise damage the plants the gardener has carefully tended and grown, whether ornamental or vegetable. Coddling moths, slugs and snails, leatherjackets, pigeons after the peas, blackbirds after the raspberries or pulling up the newly planted bulbs or onions, blackfly on the beans, whitefly in the greenhouse, rabbits in the salad, squirrels in the trees, caterpillars eating the cabbages – the list is vast.

Many of these can be dealt with most effectively by prevention, barriers, stopping the critters getting at the pants in the first place. Netting, fine meshes, fruit/vegetable cages, grease barriers, all these are far more effective than poisons. The humble slug/snail pub does a very effective job. Even if you go in for nematodes you'll find you still need slug pubs to deal with the already grown adults the nematodes won't get to. I prefer this method to nematodes for cost reasons as well.

Sometimes things can get serious very quickly, as with aphids, so that you have to use soft soap to kill them or the plants will die, you can't wait for the more usual organic methods to work. Biodynamics doesn't deny you this ability, nobody wants your plants to die.

However, thinking ahead really does help. I get my slug pubs going as soon as I start to work outside which can be January or February here depending on the weather. I don't wait for the baby slugs to get to adult size ... and begin breeding to produce even more of the little darlings to eat my hostas and brassicas. All the brassicas live inside mesh tunnels to make it impossible for the butterflies to get to the leaves to lay their eggs so, with a reasonable amount of care, no caterpillars get to them.

I also plant lots of nasturtiums which the caterpillars like even better, and leave a couple of cabbages outside the net so they have something to eat and we do have more butterflies next year.

It's all a question of balance, of give and take. I want to take from the land in the form of beauty, i.e., hostas, dahlias, etc. so I give back to the land and her creatures with some plants for them to feed on. Usually this works out, unless the weather is very bad with lots of summer rain to encourage the slugs, or some other factor comes into play. I win some, I lose some. In the long term both Nature and myself get what we need.

Rats

One creature that can really be a problem is the rat. Wherever you are on planet Earth you are never more than a couple of meters away from a rat. Rats and people have been close neighbours for as long as there have been humans. The rats, of course, are a far older species than we, goodness knows what they cuddled up to before we came along. Modern human living suits rats to a T, they really thrive on our wasteful culture. And we are generally terrified of them ... a problem we've brought on ourselves.

The best way to tell if you have a rat problem is if you see them. If you see rats around then there are too many, they are getting hungry and are much braver in consequence so they come out when people are around rather than stay hiden. The milder winters we've had for some time now mean they don't die off in the cold so there are more of them to start over again each spring. That happens with slugs and snails too, by the way ... the milder climate means they live longer!

Whatever, rats are a problem, they do need to be kept under control and out of the compost heap. If you begin to see rats then you need to take steps to cull them, or have someone do this for you. The farmers' stores have poisons that will do this or you can contact your local authority to sort them out for you. Most effective of all are the terrier-men; terriers will hunt and kill rats extremely quickly and effectively, they're kinder than poison.

Note – if you put poison down make quite sure it can't be eaten by other creatures you don't want to cull, like your cat or dog! So keep a very close eye on your own pets. Modern rat poisons work more slowly than the old ones and tend to make the animal drowsy, watch your pets, they might eat a rat or mouse that's been poisoned. If you suspect this take your pet to the vet immediately and ask for tests. Vitamin K can counteract the poison and save your pet's life but you must act quickly.

And – over the past few years many people have seen rats climbing onto bird tables and eating the seed and nuts. Some of the bird foods are rich in vitamin K, with the consequent result that the rats who eat it develop a resistance to the poison! Ho hum! We do make rods for our own backs, don't we, so long as we look only to cure an effect rather than seeking the cause.

A biodynamic way of dealing with rats is to make a pepper – see the section on Peppers – but handling rats is dangerous, even when they're dead, because of the diseases you can unfortunately catch from them. We have used a rat-pepper and it does work, however it takes much longer than using poison so I don't work that way if the problem is big. If we have an explosion in the rat population due to a mild winter then I get the rat-poison out.

Rats in Compost Bins

Keeping rats out of the compost heap is best done by putting a layer of mesh – plasterer's mesh, as it's called in the UK – underneath the bins. This is sufficiently fine so that even baby rats can't get through, but the worms and bugs that do so much good in your heap can.

Go to a builders' yard and ask for plasterers' mesh, buy enough to go under your bin(s). Lay it on the ground where the bin is going to be and stake the mesh down into the ground or weight it down with bricks. Put the bin(s) back on top of the mesh and fix them to the mesh so the rats can't move them. Make compost as normal.

We always do this with all our bins, whether or not we see any rats. We know they're there, and that they will go into the bins if they can, so we use prevention in the form of the mesh.

Weeds

Weeds tell you things about the soil, about excesses and deficiencies. There are some good books on the subject that are well worth reading as they will help you understand what's going on with your garden. Some weeds, like nettles, really improve any soil they've been growing in. So, while you're heaving them out of the bed you want to put roses or cabbages in, don't forget to thank them for the fine, crumbly earth you now have to work with. It's also full of nutrients left by the nettles. The occasional oath as you get stung is quite in order too.

However, sometimes weeds just get too numerous, they show an imbalance that needs something more than weeding and using the preparations ... this is where you use the Peppers.

Peppers

These are homeopathic-like preparations – the peppers are not homeopathy – that we make to deal with occasional imbalances. They work on both pests and weeds.

The peppers are, I think, similar to the concepts behind homeopathy – treating like with like, which is called "the law of similars". You may already use homeopathy and so have some idea of this. In homeopathy you use belladonna, for instance, to help fevers as one of the symptoms of belladonna – taken straight – is fever, so you cure fever with the essence of a fever-producing plant.

Taking this idea, you use slugs to deter slugs, rabbits to deter rabbits, docks to deter docks. You make a preparation out of the weed or pest itself, then spray this around the plants or area of the garden you want to protect, or the whole garden itself.

The simplest prep to start with is slugs – there are a couple of ways of doing this.

Slug-Soup

Make slug-soup and spray it around the plants you wish to protect from the slugs.

Begin by catching a good tub full of slugs. Go out with a torch and a bucket, very early in the morning or at night, especially if it's been raining or where you've watered. Look under stones, plant pots, on the lawn, you'll soon get a bucket-full.

When you have a good half-bucket of the things dump them in water with a little salt in it so they die. Put a lid on it and leave it for three days. The result with be a disgusting smelling liquid – do not go look just after eating!

Take the liquid, dilute it 1-3, and spray it around the area you are protecting. The slugs (understandably) don't like this and will stay away.

Slug Pepper

The method is basically the same for any weed or pest …

Get 50+ dead slugs; or a pile of the weed; or the skin of a pest like a squirrel or rabbit. Use something like an old barbeque for the burning and reduce the dead slugs, (or weed or animal skin) to ashes. Grind the resulting ash in a pestle and mortar for an hour – this is called dynamising. Spread the resulting, dynamised, powder around the area to be protected; this will deter the pest or weed for the whole season.

For weeds like docks, thistles, ground elder, bindweed even, you can either burn the whole plant or just the seeds.

To make the peppers extra effective work with the star calendar. Maria Thun gives dates which are best for making various peppers but I do them on other dates because I'm desperate to deal with the problem and the relevant date is months off. They still work. They're even more effective when you can work with the calendar but it's better to do something when it's needed than to be pedantic in following the "rule-book" and often the dates for making the pepper are not at all when you actually need the thing.

Doing hands-on biodynamics, discovering for yourself that it works, is the best way of learning. Don't head into the theory and boil your brain with indigestible ideas before you've seen the reality for yourself. It's much easier to understand something when you've actually done it, seen it for yourself, than just read about it. That's why scientists do experiments, and cooks make practical dishes before they write the recipes! You do it, then your brain is able to handle the theory. Not the other way about.

Diseases

Disease come from imbalance in the ecosystem of your garden so the biodynamic answer, again, is to get in balance using the preparations. It certainly isn't an instant method nor a quick dose of weed killer as advertised on TV. Biodynamics works at the causes of a problem not doing a quick-fix on the presenting symptom.

As well as using the preparations and the peppers, there are various teas you can make that help restore balance and so counteract diseases.

508 – Equisetum Tea

Equisetum, horsetail, tea is used to control fungal problems. We find it most effective if done on three consecutive days.

Horsetail is an ancient, prehistoric plant and an invasive weed in the wrong places. Like the ferns and mosses that came before the sexually pollinated plants, it is a spore-bearing rather than a flowering plant that came before flowers and sexual reproduction evolved in plants. As well as its spores, horsetail also develops a network of rhizomes well below even double digging depth and even the tiniest bit of chopped rhizome will grow into a new plant. The summer shoots look like small trees ... horsetail was trees in the carboniferous period.

I stood in a field of them once in southern France, in the dawn when the dew was on them, it was quite eerie and fae as well as very beautiful. However, later over breakfast, I did wonder how the locals felt about them as they had made the land pretty well unusable for anything else, including forest.

If you live in an area where they are prevalent, like that field in France, you may want to make the prep yourself – and a pepper to try to get rid of it! But most of us buy the dried plant from our local/national BD association rather than risk getting the stuff in the garden! It's as bad as Japanese Knotweed.

To make it, simmer 20g of the bought preparation in 1litre of water for about an hour. Dilute 5-10 times and use as a spray on plants affected by any fungal condition, including black spot on roses and various mildews. It's very good for fungal problems with trees.

Nettle Tea

Nettles are amazing plants that actually condition the soil they grow in – even if they sting us to death when we pull them out of places they aren't wanted! But they are wonderful soil condi-toners, the earth they leave us with is marvellous for growing.

We always add fresh, chopped nettles to the compost heaps, as well as using the nettle compost preparation. They help enormously.

Nettle tea has two main uses ... first as an insecticide for aphids and second as a foliar feed. The one process makes both.

To make it, take 1k of nettles to a ten gallon bucket of water. Chop the nettles up and put in the bucket. Cover with the 10 gallons of water. Put a lid or cover on the bucket and leave for 24 hours.

The following day you'll have the insecticide. You can spray this onto the plants without dilution; it's an excellent preparation to spray onto all plants affected by aphids, this includes black fly on broad beans.

If you leave the preparation for a week you have an excellent foliar feed – but you'll need a clothes peg on your nose for the smell, it's worse than comfrey juice! Dilute the feed 1-10 and spray onto the plants. All plants can benefit from it.

Tree Paste

Tree paste is invaluable for all trees, fruit, flowering, woodland. It's worth doing every year, your trees will be healthier and crop better. Decorative trees, coppice and woodland show a big difference as quickly as after the first year of application; health, vitality, flowering and seasonal colour are all improved. Large areas of woodland need a lot of labour to do the job but it's only once a year and the results make it well worth organising.

Again, tree paste is something you have to make yourself as it doesn't keep – like the preparations. It's hard work and definitely a time to invite friends to help and share in the proceeds.

You need ...
- 5 builders' buckets of fresh cow dung

- 500 g (18oz) of finely ground basalt- you can buy this already ground, often called rock dust
- 2 builders' buckets of ground up dried clay – as we live on clay soil we get this from when we clear the beds; any clay we find as we dig out we put to one side and save. If you don't have clayey ground this is something you'll have to beg from neighbours or buy in.
- A hard-surface space to work
- Heavy-duty plastic sheeting or hardboard to save the work surface
- A clock – preferably with an alarm
- 3 friends with spades – ask them to bring their own bucket (and spades) to take their tree paste home in.
- Lots of tea and cake

Method

Cover the hard surface to stop staining. Put the dung onto it and add the clay and basalt – think enormous cake-mix!

Now, you have to "stir" for an hour – this means cutting and turning the dung-clay-basalt mix with a spade to mix it thoroughly so do the Tree-Paste Dance (spading) ... take the spade and push it into the mix, lift out a spade-full and turn it over onto the heap. Take a step round the heap and do it again. And again, and again!

Each person spades the mix for five minutes, then the next person and so on for the hour. Work round the heap in a circle – spade-turn-step, spade-turn-step. Those not spading can enjoy tea and cake, and keep the kettle boiling!

As you work, watch the mixture change, becoming a really well stirred heap, combining all the ingredients fully. When the hour's up the mix is ready to go onto the trees. Share it out between you, each take some home for your own trees.

You paint the trunk of the tree on all sides, covering it thinly but well, for a couple of feet up from the ground. The tree trunk absorbs the paste over the following months, getting the goodness, and shows its appreciation over coming seasons.

The mixture doesn't keep for very long so don't spend too much time after on that cake and tea! You need to apply it within about three-four hours of making. And you need to make it new each year – you can't save any for later.

Just using the preparations several times a year brings the land into balance. As you get into the habit of this you'll find the need to use corrective methods such as peppers, teas and pastes becomes less and less necessary. The land is in good heart, in harmony with itself, with the plants that grow there, and the animals, birds and insects that live there ... and with you and your needs, the way you work. You are a team, working together, fulfilling all your needs and aims.

Chapter 10

Making the Preparations

Let me reiterate straight away that you don't need to make any of the preps yourself; you can buy them already to stir or put into your heap from your local/national biodynamic association – see the appendix for contacts. However, you may decide you want to make the preps for yourself, or at least some of them, the two horn preps are possible for anyone so inclined even in a small town garden.

I think it's important that people know, if they wish to, how all the preps are made. It's not "black magic" even if the methods are unusual. I don't propose to attempt much on why you do it this way, or why it works, that's certainly beyond me and I think beyond anyone else at the present time. As I've said before, there are many things we do without knowing all the whys and wherefores. We know they work, that they do what we want, and biodynamics is (at the moment) like that, although I suspect there will come a time when we are able to explain some of the whys. Evolution works like that, going from the experiential to the theoretical ... not the other way about!

And let me say again that no animals are ever slaughtered just to make the preparations. All the animal components come from animals that are being slaughtered for food in any case. In biodynamics we use everything we possibly can of every beast killed – waste is inimical to BD and is considered cruel as well.

Cow-Pat-Pit (aka Barrel Prep)

This is such a valuable preparation, I wouldn't be without it for the world. For gardeners, especially in town with small gardens, making compost has to be a different thing than for farmers and big places like the RHS gardens, Kew or the National Trust.

Ordinary gardeners mostly have to compost in layers – and this is true for everyone who has kitchen waste to deal with. Kitchen waste turns up every day as we cook and eat, even in a restaurant, you can't stack it up to wait until you have a big heap as it becomes very unpleasant.

As you saw in the chapter on composting, working in layers, cold heap composting, is different to using big heaps or bins that are left for months to cook. Layer composting doesn't build up so great heat and works in different ways. We use starter preparations for use with cool heaps, including bokashi bins and wormeries. Cow-pat-pit, also known as barrel prep, is one I use. It's a very easy and cheap DIY starter you can make for yourself if you have access to cowpats and a bit of space in your garden to make the pit, as well as the time and energy to make it.

You can use it straight onto the garden itself, as an extra booster, as well as in the bins.

You need ...

- The six compost preparations
- 5 buckets of fresh cow dung
- 100g (4 oz) of eggshells (organic or free-range – you don't want all the antibiotics, steroids and muck poor battery hens have been fed in the food from your garden). We save the shells from the eggs we eat during the year, they're very easy to crush to a fine dust and stored in a box in the fridge.
- 500 g (18oz) of finely ground basalt
- An old bottomless barrel about half a meter deep buried into the ground, with a lid
- an old dustbin with the bottom cut off is good for this, or an old fruit-juice barrel of the sort you can use for collecting rainwater – they're often available free from the juice factories.
- A hard-surface space to work

- Heavy-duty plastic sheeting or a piece of old hardboard to cover the work area
- A clock – preferably with an alarm
- 3+ friends with spades (share the prep between you) and … lots of tea and cake for afters

Cover the hard surface to stop staining. Put the dung onto it and sprinkle with the crushed eggshells and basalt. (The preps go in last)

Now you have to "stir" for an hour – so set the alarm clock, as with the tree paste. This is why you need the friends. Stirring in this case means cutting and turning the dung-eggshell-basalt mix with a spade to mix it thoroughly.

Spading: Do the Tree-Paste Dance again … the Cow-Pat-Pit dance now! Take the spade and push it into the mix. Lift out a spade-full and turn it over onto the heap. Take a step round the heap and do it again. And again, and again!

Each person spades the mix for five minutes, then the next person and so on for the hour. Work round the heap in a circle – spade-turn-step, spade-turn-step. Being completely nuts in this household we often find ourselves making up and singing daft songs as we work. Singing, of course, is not compulsory! But we find it makes the work more fun.

Those not spading can enjoy their tea and cake – keep the kettle boiling for more after you've all done!

As you work, watch the mixture change to become a really well stirred heap combining all the ingredients fully. When the hour's up the mix is ready to go into the bottomless barrel.

Now you need to stir the valerian (prep 507) for twenty minutes.

Take half a bucket of warmed water (blood heat) and put about twenty drops of prep 507 into it, then stir for twenty minutes. Use the trusty bucket and broom-handle from your other stirrings.

As always, you make a vortex down to the bottom of the bucket going clockwise, take the pole out and watch the vortex rise to the top again, then put the pole in and create a vortex going the other way (anticlockwise).

Repeat this for twenty minutes – say 5 minutes each. Share the stirring between you, less effort and more companionable (you're probably really looking forward to that tea and cake by now!).

When the prep 507 is stirred put it into a watering can with a rose – you water it onto the contents of the pit last of all.

Now you've got the solid mix and the liquid valerian ready, it's time to fill that pit with the mixture you've stirred.

Shovel in half the mixture. Then put in half of one unit of each of the five solid compost preps into the mixture in the same pattern as you would in a "hot heap" compost bin. Now, water over half the prep 507

Put the rest of the dung mix in the pit and put the other half of each of the five solid compost preps in. Water over with the last of the 507, valerian. Your pit is done.

Put the lid on and leave it for a month. Then open it up, give it a stir around and put it back to sleep again for another four weeks.

After these eight weeks, your cow-pat-pit prep is ready for use so you can ladle it out and put it into storage jars. Share the jars between you all who did the stirring. Store the glass jar, labelled and with a loose fitting to let in air in, in constant temperature, in a cool dark place.

If you live in a town, have gardening neighbours, are a member of a garden club or allotment group, why not get together a group of interested people and make the cow-pat-pit preparation as a group?

And this is how it's possible for us all to buy the preps rather than having to make them. Folk like us make some extra and the biodynamic association sells it on for cost only – no profit involved here, just goodwill and sharing. You could join in and give some of your prep for others to use.

The Spray Preps

If you live in a town, have gardening neighbours, are a member of a garden club or allotment group, why not get together a group of interested people and make the spray preparations as a group? You'll need about 1-2 horns per person and just the one pit between you all. it's like doing neighbourhood composting or gardens. It's good fun doing the work in a group as well as sharing the labour.

As with the cow-pat-pit ... this is how it's possible for us all to buy the preps rather than having to make them. Folk like us make some extra and the biodynamic association sells it on for cost only – no profit involved here, just goodwill and sharing. You could join in and give some of your prep for others to use.

You can buy horns – at cost, no profit – from your local biodynamic association: see contacts.

500 – Horn Manure

This is cow manure which has been buried in a cow's horn from autumn to spring equinox.

All of nature, including us humans, are energy-consuming beings. When food is digested it gets broken down into its component parts. As it passes through the digestive tract it gets processed by the juices of the mouth, oesophagus, stomach and small and large intestines. All of these body-parts are able to absorb nutrient from the food as it goes through the process which turns the food back into energy again – as it was originally, in the form of sunlight – so our body-cells can use it. Neither we nor any animal actually uses the food, solid matter that we eat. We use the energy our digestive systems are able to obtain from it. This energy is measured in calories, the calorie is a measure of energy, we use and consume energy.

Cows produce the very best manure, partly because of their size and diet as well as their temperament. They also have some forty to forty-five meters of digestive tract – that's an awful lot! – which handles the almost continuous eating that cows, kept properly, are built to do. But the most important fact about them – in terms of prep 500 – is their four stomachs.

All ruminant animals – cows, goats, sheep, deer – have very long digestive tracts and four stomachs. The word ruminant is about chewing the cud, likely you'll have noticed how cows and sheep will stand or lie chewing quietly in the field, this is chewing the cud and a vital part of the huge digestive process these animals use. All ruminants are also cloven hoofed and naturally have horns. Modern insurance practices and rules try to insist that farmers cut the horns off their cattle or disbud them when they are new-born calves. Biodynamics does not go along with this and all biodynamic cows have their horns.

Cows don't naturally have three meals a day – they eat all the time, slowly walking across their pasture, biting off grass and herbs and chewing the cud. Unfortunately, because of economics, greed and the massive demand for milk, cows on industrial farms are fed about three times a day so their digestive tract doesn't work as nature intended. The physical and emotional strain of being forced to eat when the human says so, being treated as a unit of production, despite the fact that your body was built for continuous input must be pretty bad for cows that live in deep litter for most of their lives, as many do on industrial farms. This stress has knock-on effects on the milk they produce and our health if we drink it, likely it's a contributory cause of the massive dairy allergies current at the moment. Ditto butter and cheese produced from the milk too.

On biodynamic and organic farms cows have food available to them all the time, in fields as much as possible and with continuously filled hay/straw racks when they are in deep litter, so their guts work as they are supposed to. As a consequence they produce superb manure for us to use in the garden and on the farm ... and to make Prep 500 with.

You make this preparation around the time of the Autumn equinox.

You need ...

- Cows' horns – you'll need at least three or four. If you're going to do it why not get several and share the results with friends and your local garden club and/or biodynamic group? You'll need 1-2 horns per person depending on the size of their land, we use 4+ horns per year here on our quarter acre. You can buy horns from your local biodynamic association – see contacts.
- Cow pats – freshly gathered from the field a day or so before you want to fill the horns. Make sure you have permission from the farmer to be on her/his land! Get cow pats that are stiff rather than sloppy in constituency. It helps if the farmer has fed hay for a week or two before you collect the dung.
- Rubber gloves
- Old long-handle tea spoon and a piece of bent coat-hanger
- A Pit to bury the horns in, it should be about half a meter both deep and wide to accommodate the horns.

Ensure the pit gets a good dollop of sunlight each day, as well as some shade and that the rain can get to it as well. It needs the four elements – earth, air, fire (sunlight) and water to process properly. This is important for both 500 and 501 preparations.

Find a place that will never be disturbed as you will be using the pit year-in-year-out for both the spray preparations. It can be decorative and doesn't have to look like a bit of old field but make sure the elements can get to it. It shouldn't be infested with tree or shrub roots – and digging around the roots twice a year won't do any good to the trees either. It shouldn't be near a wall, road or ditch. If the soil is clayey, wet or impermeable it's a good idea to dig a drain for the pit.

Method

Stuff the horns with the cow pat making sure it fills up all the way down. This is where the teaspoon and bent coat-hanger come in, poking the stuff with an old spoon or bent wire helps move it down and takes out air bubbles that stop it filling the horn.

When all the horns are full bury them in the pit. You put the horns into the pit open-end down and points up to stop water draining into them and wrecking the preparation. Then you refill in around and between the horns with good topsoil and leave them there over the winter.

Make sure the pit is marked in some way or you may forget where it is and spend ages come next spring hunting for it. A good idea is to mark the extent of the pit with flat tiles around the edge, sunk into the grass so that you can mow over them. It also looks good and makes a feature of the place. Our pit is in the middle of a circular lawn in a little grove.

The finished product ...

You leave the horns in the pit until just after the spring equinox, or even longer depending on the weather. Good spring sunshine helps for the final weeks.

Remove the horns from the pit and refill it loosely, so you can easily dig it out again if you are going to make prep 501. Stack the horns outside under shelter and leave for two or three days to dry out. Then remove the preparation by knocking the horns gently together, open end down, over a bucket. The contents should fall out but a bent coat-hanger will get bits out of the corners.

Store the preparation in glass jam jars with lids loosely screwed on so a little air can get in, or you can put several layers of muslin over the top held on with an elastic band, like homemade jam. Or you can spend lots of money on the special earthenware pots most BD associations sell. The latter are very nice but glass jars work perfectly well and come for free with the jam in our house.

You need sphagnum moss to surround the jars and a box to put them in. The jars should be completely surrounded in the sphagnum moss to retain the atmosphere they need, and the lids should be only loosely screwed on so air and moisture can get into the jars.

When you dig them up, the contents of the horns should be dark brown with no smell of manure, only the pleasant scent of humus. If the contents are wet, green or smelling of manure, the horns are not ready and the most likely cause is that the cow pats were too wet. You can leave them in the pit for a few more weeks to mature.

A wooden box is probably the most convenient, it will be solid and cool and dark as required. Some people, who make a lot of preparations, build an outdoor box against the wall of a shed or garage out of concrete blocks, with a waterproof lid. This is fine, it fulfils all the criteria of dark, solid, safe, frost-free and retaining moisture. If you're into DIY it's a good idea.

501 – Horn Silica

This is ground quartz, silica – quartz crystal – which has been buried in a cow's horn from midsummer to autumn equinox.

Quartz crystal, silica, makes up the largest proportion of minerals on the surface of our planet, 47% of the Earth's crust. It also forms an appreciable part of the bodies of plants, particularly grasses and horsetails, and is necessary to the skin, eyes and nerves in animals and people. Plants take it up in colloid form – see Thoughts: colloids. There is a lot of finely dispersed silica spread about in the atmosphere too but plants find this more difficult to absorb.

As crystal, it's very beautiful stuff, catching and reflecting light, and has been valued for millennia for its beauty as well as other qualities. In biodynamics it focuses and amplifies light and warmth energy (including infra-red and all the other parts of the electromagnetic spectrum) for the plants and the land. This helps plants grow to their true potential.

If you have crystal in your garden naturally, and quite often people do, then it's especially good to grind up your own and use that for your prep 501. You don't need much each year, one horn will keep the average town garden going for a year or three.

Again, why not make extra and share it around, through your garden club or allotment, and through your biodynamic association?

You make this prep in the month before midsummer.

You need ...

- Ground quartz crystal – in the form of fine dust, like flour. It's hard work to grind up yourself but there may be someone in your area who does grinding who could do this for you. Make sure the equipment is clean and won't contaminate your crystal. Or buy it ready ground from your local BD association.
- Cow horns – available from your local BD association
- Rain water
- The same pit you had your prep 500 horns in – having removed and emptied those horns, of course!

Note: you can't use horns that have been used for making 501 again for 501 so you have to get new horns for this each year. You can use them for making 500 though, and keep reusing them for the horn manure prep.

Method

Make a paste of the rainwater and the floury silica powder, it should be just on the point of being runny but not quite.

Fill the cow horn(s) – a good idea is to stand them up in a box of sand so the mouth is level, and the point down in the sand. Fill them right up to the brim.

Leave for twenty-four hours, after which the silica will have settled. Pour off the small amount of water left on the top and refill to the brim again with silica paste.

When the silica is fairly dry and has turned solid cover the mouths of the horns with damp clay soil and bury in the pit, point upwards as for horn manure to keep the rain out.

The finished product ...

Leave the horns to "cook" in the soil warmed by the summer sun until the autumn equinox when you dig them up.

Empty the horns and keep the preparation in a glass jar, with a good screw lid, and keep it on the window ledge in the sunlight. This is the one preparation that doesn't go into the box.

The Compost Preparations

You need space between these preparations while they do their stuff.

Unfortunately, this means you need quite a lot of acreage to make all the preps in one year. It's usually biodynamic farmers or people with very large gardens who can do this as they have the space. They make extra preps, more than they need for themselves, the surplus goes to the association for selling on to us who don't have the space. It's non-profit work, we are only charged a small amount that covers the admin and postage.

However, if you can make just one of the compost preps, and send some on to the BD association as well as sharing it with gardening friends, then it helps add to the general store.

502 – Yarrow

This is yarrow flowers that have been put into the bladder of a red deer stag at spring equinox which is hung in a dry, sunny place until autumn equinox; the bladder is then buried over winter and dug up in spring. This preparation takes a whole year to make.

Yarrow, Achillea millefolium, is a pretty and popular garden plant now. The natural wild stuff, with the white flowers, is most commonly used for the preparation. Unless you have a very big acreage you won't be able to grow enough flowers – at least not without giving up everything else which probably rather defeats your object – so you'll have to get them from your local BD association. In Britain all wild flowers are protected so they are not harvested to extinction, to the detriment of the wildlife, so you can't collect flowers from the wild.

The other half of this preparation, the container, is the bladder of a red deer stag. This is the animal component, as the cow horns were for preps 500 and 501. Over eighty years of work and recording has found that the stag's bladder and the yarrow make the right mix for this preparation. Other containers have been tried but the preparation just doesn't work in them, nature needs the stag + yarrow combination to make this preparation.

You can get a stag's bladder from deer farms after the cull if you are happy to process it yourself, after all, it's not that different from doing the Sunday joint. It's good to know where your food – including the compost preps for your veg plot – come from.

If you get the bladder yourself you need to blow it up, fill it with air, as soon as possible after it's removed from the carcass so it doesn't stick together and become unusable. You can use it fresh or dry it by hanging it in the air within some form of protection to stop birds and mice trying to eat it – after all, it's good food to them! When it's dry, store it in a cool, dry place, again safe from hungry mice, etc. Make sure bladders don't get frosted.

You begin making this preparation just after the spring

equinox. It takes a whole year to make. You do the second part of the making at the autumn equinox.

You need ...

- Yarrow flowers – tell the BD association how many bladders you intend to fill and they will give you the right quantity of dried yarrow flowers.
- Stag's bladder – again available from you BD association.
- Freshly squeezed yarrow juice and/or yarrow-flower tea
- Sausage-filling funnel
- Spoon or smooth, rounded stick

Method

Collecting your own – Yarrow flowers are collected on sunny flower days and when the flowers are fully open. Use the florets and try to remove all the stalks if you can – a fiddly process! As the yarrow flowers will not be out for spring equinox in most places you need to have *picked and dried them the previous year*. Dry the bunches of yarrow flowers by hanging them up in the air in a shed. You pick them one summer then store them by hanging them up until the following year when you make the preparation.

You can buy the yarrow flowers ready to go from the BD association.

Whether you've collected your own or bought them in you now need to spray the dried florets with freshly squeezed yarrow juice or a combination of fresh juice and tea made from the dried flowers; this is to bring the moisture level back to that of freshly wilted plants.

Stuff the moistened flowers into the stag's bladder.

To do this you'll need to cut a hole about two fingers in width in the cartilaginous opening of the bladder; a sausage-filling funnel is useful to get the material in and a spoon handle or a smooth rounded stick to stuff it down. The filled bladder should have its natural spherical form and be well but not excessively stuffed to avoid splitting when it dries.

Tie the hole closed firmly with string that won't break and make a loop of the end to hang the bladder from. Hanging the bladder in an onion net is an even better idea then the bladder doesn't take the strain and is very unlikely to break.

It also helps to hang the bladder, in the onion net, within a cage of wire netting or your birds may think it's the latest thing in fat balls and peck it open! Make sure the netting is small enough mesh to keep out tiny tits and wrens, and far enough from the bladder that little beaks can't reach through.

Hang the bladder in the sun but under cover from rain for the whole summer.

After the autumn equinox take the bladder down and bury it in a pit about half a meter deep.

Unfortunately, you can't use the horn pit and the bladder pit mustn't be near the horn pit either – this is one of the reasons small gardens can't accommodate making all the preps, not enough space. Each of the preps needs space between it and any others so they're usually made on farms or in large gardens.

Line the bladder pit with freshly cut elder branches to protect the bladder from mice eating it. Mice, like most of us, don't like the smell of cut elder!

Add a thin layer of soil then put the bladder(s) on that; if you have more than one bladder make sure they're not touching.

Fill the pit with loose soil so all the bladders are encased in earth, then cover with a piece of clean, natural-fibre sacking.

Put more elder over the top and some old roofing slates, a piece of hardboard or something to stop you busting the bladders with the spade when you come to dig them up next year.

Finally fill up the pit with earth and don't forget to mark it!

You dig up the bladder(s) the following spring – carefully, so you don't break them. This is a bit like an archaeological dig. The slates or hardboard should stop you spading them and the remains of the sacking and the elder branches will mark the boundary between the soil and the place where the bladders are, but the bladders will be disintegrating.

When you come to the boundary stop using the spade and get in there with your fingers and a spatula. In most cases only the outline of the bladder and fragments of the membrane will remain. Rather than lose any of the flower preparation take up a bit of the soil with it as well – it will all look like very good tilth!

Store the preparation in a glass jar, in your preparation box – marked with its name and date, like jam! You can use it straight away. The bladder pit can be used again and again – but only for this preparation! – if you want.

503 – Chamomile

This is chamomile that has been put in the small intestine of a cow, at midsummer, and hung in an airy, shady place until autumn equinox.

The chamomile you use for the preparations is Matricaria recutita, with dense, bushy growth, finely divided leaves and widely divided shoots terminating in a yellow flower head with white ray florets and characteristic scent. It flowers all through summer and its fine roots break up compacted soil giving structure to the topsoil.

The other half of this preparation, the container, is a cow's small intestine. This is the animal component for this preparation and, as with the yarrow prep, eighty-plus years of work and research has shown the cow's intestine and the chamomile together make the right mix for this preparation.

You can get cows' intestine, ready for use, from your national biodynamic association. If you want to do the whole process yourself then ask at the local abattoir if you can get them there; however you may not be able to because of the various laws on what has to be done with animal organs due to mad cow disease.

The intestine from the BD association will come with instructions on how to store it until it's time to make the prep. It will be dried, not frozen as this isn't good for it.

This preparation is made at midsummer, ready for the autumn equinox.

You need ...

- Chamomile flowers
- Chamomile tea made from the fresh, whole, plants
- A cow's small intestine
- Sausage-filling funnel
- Spoon or smooth, rounded stick
- 2 large, unglazed earthenware flower pots

Chamomile flowers have a longish flowering period, usually beginning in early summer. It's best to pick the flowers in the morning of a flower day, and as you need large quantities to fill a cow's intestine you'll be collecting over several weeks. As with the other flowers, you can't pick them from the wild in Britain so unless you have a large area to grow them you'll need to get them from your local BD association.

If you have your own dry the flowers on a wire tray or on paper right after picking. Store the dried flowers in paper bags which can breathe, let the air through them, in a dry shady place, a shed will do.

Method

Take the dried flowers and wet them with the chamomile tea.

Take the cow's intestine, tie off one end. Fit the other end onto the sausage funnel, make sure it's tight so it won't slip off.

Use the smooth stick to push the plant material through the funnel into the intestine – it's just like making sausages.

Hang the intestine up to dry in the shed for a few days. If you bury it while wet it will rot more quickly and attract mice and other small animals to eat it.

Place the intestine, enclosed in the pair of unglazed flower pots mouth-to-mouth to keep the mice out and stop you accidently slicing the intestine or bladder with your spade when you come to dig them up. The pots being unglazed allows air to permeate through the pots.

Bury the intestines in a pit similar to the one for the yarrow – but not the same pit! Again, you can't use the same pit as you do for the horn preparations, each prep needs its own space.

Line the pit with elder again to keep away the mice.

The following spring, dig up the chamomile sausages. Crumble the remains – bits of intestine and all – and store in a glass jam jar, in the preparation box, surrounded by sphagnum moss as you do for the other preparations. Don't forget to mark it with the date you made it.

504 – Nettle

This is nettles which are cut at their flowering time and buried in the earth for a whole year.

Peacock butterflies and small tortoiseshells lay their eggs on nettles so their caterpillars can feed on them. Nettles are worthwhile in lots of ways. Nettle soup, made with a bit of spinach, fried onions and garlic, some coconut milk and pine nuts is delicious. Some people add a bit of ginger to the mix for extra spice. Nettle tea as a rinse for the hair gives a marvellous shine, and is a good tonic tea as well. Nettles are also an excellent insect repellent for aphids and a good foliar feed too. The Romans used to beat themselves with nettles to help rheumatism. As a sufferer of rheumatoid arthritis I've never found nettle stings any help at all! However others might.

Soil that has had nettles growing in it becomes a wonderful fine tilth. Nettles do the soil a lot of good, they improve the soil structure, remove excess nitrogen and iron. Of course, we don't want them competing in veg and flower beds but, as they say, a weed is only a plant in the wrong place.

The nettle preparation, 504, doesn't use an animal organ for its container. The nettles lie within sacking, in a layer of peat, in the soil in yet another pit. This pit, too, needs to be well away from the other pits – you can see why you need a lot of land to make the preps.

Just think what archaeologist will make of all these pits dug apparently randomly across the field and filled with strange things! As all archaeologists seem to turn to religion and ritual when they don't know what something is for you can bet they'd do the same with our BD pits!

This preparation is made after spring equinox and before midsummer.

You need ...

* A new pit
* Nettles
* Peat
* Natural-fibre sacking

Gather the nettles on a flower day in the early morning, cutting them from the base. Let them lie until the afternoon when they begin to wilt.

If the nettle colony is especially dense keep an eye out for birds' nests as you're cutting, and leave the nests alone in plenty of cover. Leave some nettles for the butterflies too.

Dig the pit and line it with 5cm of peat. Line the peat with a layer of natural-fibre sacking. Lay the nettles in on top of the sacking.

When the pit is full of the nettles, cover with more sacking and cover the sacking with peat. Cover the peat with soil to the top of the pit. The nettles stay in the pit for a whole year

Dig last year's prep up in the morning after you've collected this year's batch of nettles and bottle it up in a jam jar, label and date it. Then re-line the pit with peat and sacking, in the afternoon, put the nettles in as you did before.

505 – Oak Bark

This is oak bark which is put in an animal's skull, usually a cow's or horse's skull, at the autumn equinox. The filled skull is then put in a wooden barrel, where water can run over it, until the following spring equinox.

Oak is a special and beautiful tree, its habitat is home to more insects and wildlife than any other tree. It's very long-lived. It has been, still is, a focus for many stories and folklore.

The fissured bark is what we use in prep 505. Collecting the bark must, of course, be done very carefully as the removal of too much bark causes the tree to die and we don't want this. When large amounts of preparation need to be made we go to a forester to find what trees are to be felled and ask for the bark from them. If you want to make this preparation yourself and have your own trees then you also need to know how much bark it is safe to take from a living tree unless you are having an oak felled. In BD we consider it wrong to kill trees for no reason or only to make the preparations. As with the other preps, this means you need a lot of land to grow and harvest the trees so most of us get the bark from our BD association.

If bark is taken from a living tree for prep making then that tree must also be given extra food in the form of Tree Paste.

The skull of a cow, sheep, goat, pig or horse may be the container for this preparation. Again, because of the various health and safety laws, it's impossible for an individual to get a skull from an abattoir in Britain, however your biodynamic association will be able to provide you with one or more.

This preparation is begun just before the autumn equinox then the second phase of the making begins at the spring equinox. It is finally ready in the following spring, so takes eighteen months to make.

You need ...

- A wooden half-barrel
- A drainpipe, leading off the roof of a building or greenhouse
- Stripping knife, axe or coarse file
- Oak bark
- Tough kitchen grinder, coffee grinder or mortar and pestle
- Skull

Method

If you are able to, collect bark yourself from mid-August through September. Take the bark from selected oak trees on a Root day. Bark is a part of the root of the tree and responds to being worked with on root days. Store the bark in a cool, dry place over winter.

In the spring, arrange the drainpipe so its flow will go over the barrel when it rains, there are various fittings you can get to do this. Fill the barrel up with plant waste and sludge. The barrel should have a tap in the base so the excess water can be drained off. You can use the water on the garden.

If the skull is dry soak it in water for an hour or so before you use it. This will stop cuts and abrasions from bits of dried skin left inside.

Reduce the bark to small crumbs no bigger than a pea, slightly moisten it and fill the skull with it.

If the butcher has split the skull fill the sinuses with oak bark as well; join the bony margins with a thin strand of kneaded clay and press them together; tie the two halves firmly together with wire at the front and the back. Close all the gaps with more clay.

Remove the water from the half-barrel and put the skull into the sludge. Cover with straw. When it rains the water will run through the barrel and over the skull. Drain off the water after each rainfall.

The following April take the skull out of the sludge and split it open – use a sledge hammer and wedge. Scrape out the oak bark carefully, you'll find it's now like good soil. Store it in the jam jar with its label and date.

506 – Dandelion

This is dandelions picked at spring equinox and dried over the summer. At autumn equinox they are wrapped in a cow's mesentery, buried over the winter and dug up the following spring.

Dandelions only open when the dew is gone and they feel the warmth of the sun, real sun flowers and, as a Leo, I love them. I don't pull them out of the garden unless they've snuck into one of my flower or veg beds. I'm lucky to have wild pastures and hedges where they can stay along with the other field herbs one normally pulls out of more formal gardens. In our hedges, we have bryony with its wonderful berries, dead nettles, buttercups, teasels, St John's wort, evening primrose and other bird and bee plants. Dandelions add a wonderful flash of gold to the springtime.

The mesentery is the "bag" that holds the cow's intestines separate from its other organs. It's the great fold of the peritoneum, starting at the rumen and enclosing the whole intestine like an apron on the abdominal side. It lies loose except where it is joined to the stomach.

This preparation takes a year to make. You begin the first stage in the spring, then the second stage happens in the autumn.

For the spring you need ...

- Drying tray or paper for the dandelion flowers
- Paper bags or nets to hold the drying flowers

Method

Pick the dandelion flowers early in the morning of a flower day in early spring when they are at their best. The flowers should

NOT be fully open but still in their unopened cone-shape. Flowers that have fully opened continue to ripen during drying and begin to produce seed so they should not be used; that's why you need to pick them early in the morning before the sun warms them up

Don't leave them in a container for any length of time as they will heat up and begin to rot, so becoming no good for making the preparation. Let the flowers wilt by leaving them spread in the airy shade for a few hours after picking on a drying frame of paper. Turn them a few times while they're drying to make sure they dry evenly. Store the flowers as you have the others, in paper bags or fine nets in an airy, cool place.

For the autumn you need ...

- Dandelion tea
- A pit – yes another pit!
- Sharp knife for cutting the mesentery
- Dried Dandelion flowers
- Mesentery – from your local/national BD association

Method

In the autumn, around the equinox, moisten the dried flowers with dandelion tea – there should still be dandelions about so you can make the tea from fresh flowers. You just need to make the dried flowers slightly damp the so they become like fresh flowers that have wilted, they mustn't be sodden.

Cut the mesentery into pieces about 20-35cm/side.

Put handfuls of dandelions into each square – enough to fill them to about the size of a baby's head when they are closed into a bag.

Press the flowers in firmly and fold the corners of the material around them so they're completely enclosed, then tie them up with string.

Chop up any residual mesentery and use in liquid or semiliquid manure – waste-not-want-not.

Hang the balls up to dry out a bit for two or three days. When the balls are dry, put them into the pit closed side down – as for the horns, yarrow bladders and chamomile sausages – so the water doesn't drain into them.

Line the pit with elder branches help to keep mice away.

The following spring, dig up the balls of dandelion prep and store it in its jam jar with the others.

507 – Valerian

This is the juice of the flowers that have been fermented. You do this prep all in one go when you pick the flowers.

The Valerian prep is very good for earthworms. The flowers are wonderful too, I've got a lot of the plants in the garden here, they go well in the wild hedges and the scent in June and July is wonderful. A tall, airy plant, they do well amongst things like verbena bonariensis, stipa gigantea, perovskia and Californian poppies if you want to make an ornamental see-through screen with them. They self-seed well so it's easy enough to find seedling plants the following spring to move to places you want them.

Beware! The plant spreads through rhizomes as well as seeds – that's root runners – so keep an eye out for this to stop it spreading where you don't want it. It's not a thug like the stinging nettle and creeping buttercup but it doesn't bite you when you pull it up!

The root has sedative properties in herbal medicine. The smell of the juice is one of the things some cats like! I think it's a plant you should have in the garden for its flowers and scent and beauty whether or not you choose to make the preparation.

You need ...

- Valerian flowers
- Juice extractor or press

- Large blue or brown glass bottle – dark, so the sunlight doesn't get to the juice
- Fermenting tube

Method

Pick the valerian flowers early in the morning of a flower day when they are at their best. Don't pick them all, always leave some for the insects. Otherwise take the flowers you have bought from the BD association and moisten them with a little fresh valerian tea, as you did with the dandelions, to freshen the flowers again.

Put the flowers through the juice extractor as soon as possible after picking as they will heat up if left in the container for any length of time and become no use.

Strain the green or coffee-coloured juice then decant into the bottle. Close the bottle with the fermenting tube. Excluding air helps fermentation, the tube enables the gases to escape but stops the air getting in. Don't cork it or the bottles may explode because the gases can't escape! Store in a cool dark place, like a cellar, for six weeks.

When the juice has fully fermented it will look reddish-brown in colour and have a strongly aromatic, fruity and slightly sour smell. Any that stinks or smells of manure is spoiled and should not be used as preparation. Experience has shown that picking and processing on a flower day – and definitely avoiding a leaf day – helps it not to spoil.

If you get any spoiled juice just pour it into the compost heap where it will do good and be part of the compost. It's not the preparation, so you can't use it as that, but it still has lots of plant goodness in it. It's a waste-not-want-not thing and the juice is perfectly OK for composting if not as a prep.

Chapter 11

Thoughts

Biodynamics is a very practical method of working as well as a very long word. The dictionary says the word means that part of biology which deals with vital force.

- *Bio* comes from the Greek word for life
- *Dynamic* comes from another Greek word meaning a moving force

So we could say Biodynamics is about life as a moving force used to help the growth of plants and animals. Perhaps this makes a bit more sense.

The things we do can appear weird to folk who have never considered them or worked this way. The following are some of my own thoughts, come from many years working biodynamically, reading generally and making connections.

Plants, Moon and Stars

The universe we live in is populated with zillions of stars, planets and other bodies, bundles of gas, cosmic dust clouds, all sorts of things. All these have an effect on each other, even if some of the effects seem to be so miniscule that most of us – unless we are theoretical physicists – have no inkling or interest in them. But our interest, or otherwise, doesn't stop them having their effects on each other, which ripples out to affect everything that lives on Planet Earth as well.

There are all sorts of theories about how these bodies relate to and affect each other – string theory, dark matter, curved space, dear old gravity which, although we can use, we still don't know anything much about or how and why it works. Gardening and farming experience show that biodynamics – using the preparations and working with the rhythms of the Moon, and stars – works. We don't know much about how or why in scientific terms but, like gravity, we can still use it effectively.

Earth and all the other planets are connected to the sun (our local star) by gravity, along with a host of asteroids and stuff as super engineer and inventor of the linear motor, Professor Eric Laithwaite, used to call "matter". They're all on "gravity strings" swinging around the sun in various orbits rather like a juggler keeping many balls spinning in the air. We, on Earth, are quite intimately connected to all these bodies, most closely to the moon who is held in her orbit by a gravity string to the Earth and shares the gravity string that keeps the Earth circling the sun.

The most obvious thing about the moon is that she reflects sunlight onto the Earth at night, in varying amounts, for about three weeks out of every four. But that's not the only thing she reflects.

For many thousands of years, probably going back as far as human beings began, people have seen patterns in the stars in the sky. Often the same patterns, regardless of the countries the people live in, although they may give them different names in different places. Philosophers, thinkers, priests, shamans and gardeners have all found significance in these patterns so various forms of astronomy and astrology have grown up out of them amongst human beings over the millennia.

In biodynamics, we use simple names like Ram or Goat for these star patterns rather than the Latin astrological names of Aries and Capricorn. This keeps our minds on the fact that we are looking at them as star patterns that have an effect on the Earth and the plants that grow there, rather than as astrological signs with all the human emotional inference which may not be applicable to gardening. The stars affect animals too but that's less important for gardeners than it is for farmers, unless we are lucky enough to have a few hens.

We know the moon reflects the light of the sun onto the Earth at night. Light is a form of energy, physicists call it electromagnetic energy. The visible light spectrum that we see as the colours of the rainbow is the part of this spectrum our eyes can see. But there is much more that is invisible to us yet still affects us – e.g. X-rays, ultraviolet, infrared, gamma rays and many more, including more rays and particles the physicists don't yet know much about either. The energy that helps us in biodynamics is something else for us to learn to understand better over the coming decades and may even be a part of this spectrum although nobody knows that as yet.

Although physicists know a lot about energy they would be the first to say they don't know everything. Philosophers have been telling us about energy for millennia and say it has abilities we don't yet know how to measure. In the middle ages we didn't know how to measure infrared or ultraviolet energy either but we've learned how over the years. We will learn to understand many more things, maybe even how to measure energy as the philosophers know it, in due course.

The energy I'm talking about in this book, with regard to gardening, comes under that heading – the unknown energy of the philosophers, not measurable by the sciences we know ... as yet.

The effects of doing biodynamics have been measured in many scientific studies since 1924 and lots of the results are available at *http://www.considera.org*. Even the American Department of Agriculture investigated biodynamics and found it works!

The constellations have, for millennia, been associated with what we know as the four elements – although scientists translate the word "element" very differently. These four are associated with different parts of a plant. Here's the basics again.

Soil & Roots	Leaves	Flowers	Fruits & Seeds
Earth	*Water*	*Air*	*Fire*
Bull	Crab	Twins	Ram
Virgin	Scorpion	Scales	Lion
Goat	Fishes	Waterman	Archer

Remember this diagram?

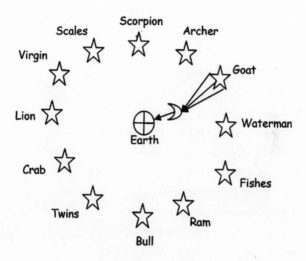

Fig 4: Moon as Lens

As the moon moves through the sky on her monthly cycle she passes in front of each of the constellations, staying in front of them for two or three days per constellation. During this period, as she passes each one, she reflects the energy of that constellation onto the Earth. Now, you may well be thinking it's only from Earth that we see these star patterns in the shapes we know, get out into space and they don't look like that at all. Very true. But ... we are talking about life on Earth, so what we see here is what we get, WYSIWYG to borrow from computer jargon. Out in space nothing works the same as it does here on earth ... of course. And that includes growing plants!

Try to take the concept of the star-energy on trust for the time being, watch it work in your own garden. The light from those stars is reaching the Earth all the time, light years from the time it left the stars in those constellations. There's more to that energy than we as yet know, are able to measure.

What I've found is that using biodynamics works, improves the soil and the growth of plants.

Why Stir?

Steiner said to stir the preps 500 and 501 for an hour and this is what we do. Why? What does the stirring do?

One of the ways homeopathic medicines are made is by stirring; it somehow puts the essence of the substance into the sugar-pill we take.

Current science hasn't yet found a way to see how there is any of the homeopathic substance in the sugar pill. As far as they can see there is nothing in the pill at all except the pill itself. But, as you may know from personal experience, homeopathy works. And it works on animals too.

Some scientists say, of humans, that it is a "placebo effect" but you cannot say that of animals. As far as we know they don't think about any medicine we give them in the ways we do. They don't know what it is, they just take it and get better. I know several vets who use it successfully with farm animals as well as domestic pets. So, even if current science cannot work out how or why it works, it still works.

Stirring is one of the methods used in making homeopathic preparations, not the most common one which is succussion where the potion is shaken but still one of the means of making the remedies.

Stirring is how we make some of the BD preps into a usable form to put on the garden.

Stirring does things to any substance that is stirred, from porridge and cake mix to biodynamic preparations. You've probably watched the transformation of a mix of oats and salt and water into a scrumptious breakfast on a winter morning. What goes into the pot isn't particularly appetising, edible yes but only if you were starving hungry and there was nothing else. What comes out of the pot makes your eyes gleam and your nose twitch as you spoon cream and honey over it. The stirring, and the heat, have transformed it.

And it's not just the heat either. If you left the pot on the stove but didn't stir you'd have a lumpy, burnt, rough-tasting mess, again not attractive nor very edible. It actually wouldn't be very digestible either although, of course, it wouldn't poison you. Your digestive tract would have trouble getting the goodness out of it, it wouldn't be in the best condition for your stomach to work on. And that's because it hadn't been stirred. Like I said, stirring does things to substances.

It transforms molecules into things called colloids.

Colloids, Clay & Cation Exchange

Colloids

A colloid is a type of mixture where one substance is dispersed evenly throughout another. Because of this dispersal, some colloids have the appearance of solutions. You'll have seen some mixtures that, when suspended in water, take many days to settle out. A particle that remains suspended in water this way, suspended but not dissolved, is called a colloid.

Organic matter forms smaller and smaller particles until it breaks down completely and still be called organic matter rather than individual elements. At this stage, just before it stops being organic matter it's called humus and humus is a colloid. When mixed with water it will not readily settle out or float to the top.

Colloidal particles are incredibly small – a teaspoon of particles has a surface area greater than a football field. Gustave Lebon in Evolution of Energy says they generate surface energies that have powerful effects on physical and chemical reactions. By the laws of physics, the smaller the particle the greater its surface area – a one-inch cube has a surface area of six square inches; the same cube divided into eight cubelets will have twice that surface area. When the cubelets become microscopic their cumulative surface area is increased enormously.

Because colloids are so small they have a huge surface area. To give you an idea of the weight to surface area ratio, clays like vermiculite have a surface area of some 800m2, that's over 200,000ft2 (like 5 acres!) per ounce!

Colloids help substances to hold structure. The colloidal state is described as the state of a solute when its molecules are not present as separate entities, as they are in a true solution, but are grouped together to form solute "particles" – read Secrets of the Soil by Tompkins & Bird for more on this. These particles are absolutely minute and detectable only by means of an ultramicroscope. They carry an electric charge, and it is their colloidal state that enables the body to absorb essential mineral elements without those essential minerals having first been processed organically by plants and animals. This is incredibly valuable to all life.

Now, all organic activities are electrical phenomena that require an ion exchange. Soil courses at horticultural colleges will tell you about this, it's one of the basics about how plants acquire food. Life, in its broadest sense, is electrical derived from the interplay of chemical elements – read The Body Electric by Robert O Becker MD for more on this. Because colloids have an extremely large ratio of surface area to the volume of material their potential to be charged with energy is extremely large too. So they enhance the electrical ability of life to be.

The larger the surface area exposed the greater the potential to be charged with energy and so their ability to absorb nutrient.

Because of colloids, the surface area of fully made humus – that is organic matter that has broken down as far as it can and still be called organic matter rather than having gone right back to its original elements – is about the same as the clay, i.e. about 800m2/ounce. Consequently it has a huge potential to carry electrical charge ... and so enable plants to feed.

Electrical charges tend to repel each other so the particles are kept separate from each other, held in suspension, retaining their vitality.

If the charge decreases the particles snap back together losing their colloidal behaviour and coagulating, becoming dead in both inorganic and organic terms.

Now, another big thought ... every cell of our body is made of colloids, arranged to perform specific functions. Nobel physicist, Wolfgang Pauli, concluded that colloids provide the most important link between the inorganic and the organic. This is a clue to the very source of life ... and biodynamics helps this link to happen ... through the stirrings.

Cations & Clay

An ion is a particle with an electrical charge.

- *Positively* charged particles are called Cations ... pronounced cat-eye-ons, emphasising the first syllable.
- *Negatively* charged particles are called Anions ... pronounced ann-eye-ons.

Having negative + positive charge together means the two particles can stick together, it's rather like static, when something nylon sticks to you. This ability to collect and hold other particles is one of the major ways nutrients are held in the soil so that plants can use them.

All organic activities are electrical phenomena that require an ion exchange and Cation Exchange Capacity – CEC – is vital to how plants get food and water.

Clay and organic matter (humus) have negatively charged sites (anions) on them that enable them to attract and hold positively charged particles (cations).

The Cation Exchange Capacity (CEC) of your soil is about how many negatively charged sites are available in it – the more the merrier because then it will attract and hold lots of positively charged cations-nutrients for your plants.

Clay soil is particularly good at this. Yes, I know, everyone groans when they hear the words clay soil but clay has the ability to hold the most nutrients of any soil and so is essential to getting a good growing medium in your garden. It does require some work from you though, to make it well able to do its job of holding nutrients and water in a form the plants can use. The work you do in adding organic matter is fundamental to Cation exchange ... and thereby the plant's ability to get nourishment from the soil.

Clay particles are incredibly tiny! They can't be seen in most microscopes. Remember what I said about surface area and colloids, and incredibly tiny particles that stay suspended in water rather than becoming a true solution? Clay particles disperse evenly through water and other substances, they're so small they can't be seen individually, they can't even be seen in most microscopes and they can take weeks or months even to settle out, or they may never settle out but remain suspended in water.

Soil is made by the geological breaking down of rocks. Heating and cooling, freezing and thawing, wind and water erosion, rain and biological activity, all these gradually break the rock down to soil, the earth's growing medium. NB – all rain is more acid than alkali which is why it's better for plants than just watering from the tap, but the excess carbon dioxide we've pumped into the air over the past 50+ years forms carbonic acid ... an unwanted and very corrosive extra. Another part of global warming.

The more rainfall a soil gets the faster it breaks down into clay. Young clays are made up of layers of silica and alumina sandwiched with either potassium or iron. They only have cation exchange sites on their edges. As the clays become "middle aged" the filling of the sandwich gets taken out by soil-life and plant roots, opening up more negatively charged exchange sites and increasing the exchange capacity. In elderly clay, the sandwich gradually gets filled up again with hydrated aluminium oxide and so loses its exchange capacity again. To help the planet, it's our job as gardeners to keep our soil's CEC high. Biodynamics helps with this.

Humus, is vital to this process ... that's about making compost. Remember, I said the surface area of just one ounce of humus is something like 5 acres, 200,000 square feet or 800 square meters. The negatively charged exchange sites increases along with the surface area, so increasing the CEC.

Organic matter of itself, dead plant material, doesn't have much cation exchange capacity, it must first be broken down into humus – this is composting. The composting process needs the action of soil microorganisms, earthworms, fungi and insects. When none of these can do anything more with the stuff, as food, it has finally become that very small but very complex carbon structure – colloid – that can hold and release many times its own weight in water and plant nutrients.

The higher the humus level the greater the exchange capacity.

The only way to increase the humus level of your soil is to make loads of compost and add it to your soil. Adding the BD preps to the compost to further increase this activity.

It took me a while, and several pots of tea, to get my head around all this but it's worth making the effort as so much gardening "science" makes a lot more sense once you do. Why we make compost, why adding organic matter to the soil is so good, all this sort of thing makes more sense once you realise the enormous effect it has.

Water, Stirring & Dr Henry Coandă

Water is strange stuff. Among its properties is an amazing ability for surface tension. For instance, if all the extraneous gases were removed from an inch thick column of water it would become harder than steel.

In the nineteen-twenties, Romanian scientist Dr Henry Coandă, father of fluid dynamics, made the apparently banal discovery that fluid flowing over any surface tends to cling to that surface as if it were alive. Physicists considered this so important it was called the "Coandă Effect". Later, Coandă found that at the centre of every snowflake is a circulatory system of tiny tubes in which still unfrozen water circulates like sap in plants or blood in animals. He considered this to be the quality of water that dowsers call "living" as opposed to stagnant.

By measuring the time it takes a snowflake to die – they die when all the water in them becomes congealed – Coandă was able to establish an extraordinary and direct relationship between the life-span of the snowflake and the life-span of peoples who regularly drink such water. The "living" fluid appeared to add more life to humans.

On his far flung travels, Coandă discovered that the water that makes long-lasting snowflakes formed a major part of the diet of many long-lived peoples. These include peoples such as the Hunza and other peoples in the Russian province of Georgia, as well as people in Peru, Ecuador and on the mountainous Tibet-Mongolian border.

When a living organism, plant or animal, takes in water it structures the water by means of colloids. The colloid particles act as tiny seeds of energy that attract free water molecules and form the nuclei of liquid crystals. The colloids require such a high electrical charge that they don't normally have to do this.

Putting this high electrical charge into the colloids is what stirring does. A vortex, or whirlpool, does this – see Podolinsky's research, working with Theodore Schwenk's ideas in Sensitive

Chaos. Such vortices exist in fast-flowing, glacial and high mountain streams like those where the Hunza people live, or in Ecuador, Peru and Tibet. Flowing water goes in layers that move against each other, flowing at different rates, so generating electrical current and charge. The water becomes colloidal, and it becomes intensely alive. Wikipedia has a good piece on the Coandă effect and its applications in science.

Stirring, Oxygen and Aerobic Bacteria

With prep 500, stirring increases the oxygen content of the prep+water by at least 70%.

With the prep 501 stirring increases the aerobic bacteria count in the silica (which is nil to begin with) goes up to some forty million bacteria (Pfeiffer's research).

Pfeiffer's spectrographic research showed several changes in the plain quartz dust. From ninety per cent silicon oxide to begin with, it somehow developed small amounts of nitrate nitrogen, magnesium, potassium, phosphates, copper, silver, alum, boron, barium, calcium, chromium and zirconium. Iron increased five times, magnesium increased one hundred times.

No-one yet knows why any this happens but it does. All these elements, in tiny trace amounts, are essential for healthy plants.

Water-holding abilityis vital for the soil. It must be able to hold water well but not become a swamp and it's calcium/magnesium ratio that determines this. It helps make the soil either tight or loose.

Tight soil (soil which has more magnesium) holds water but too tight soil, too much magnesium, becomes waterlogged. This is acid soil and it has a low breakdown of organic matter e.g. "Pete Marsh", the mummified and very well preserved druid shaman found in Britain at the end of the 20th century.

Loose soil (more calcium) has more oxygen and so more aerobic breakdown or organic matter, it is also freer draining; too loose soil lets all the water drain away. As Michael Astera says,

"If you get them [the calcium/magnesium ratio] right for your particular soil, you can drive over the garden and not have a problem with compaction".

Stirring biodynamic preps and putting them on your land helps by helping the calcium/magnesium ratio become right for your soil.

The beneficial effect of the biodynamic stirrings on plants have been witnessed by farmers and gardeners since nineteen-twenty-four. One day we will be able to understand more but, for the moment, I'm just going to keep on stirring as I love the effect it has on my garden.

Why Make the Preps This Way?

The way the preps are made is often cause for some skin-prickling amongst people new to biodynamics. Some of the methods sound like what many people think of as black magic. The Oak Bark prep is, perhaps, the most spooky as it's put into the skull of a domestic animal, usually a cow or horse. It's often the use of animal parts, skulls, horns, the mesentery bag and small intestines that spooks a lot of people ... although we use intestines to make sausages that we eat ourselves.

There is reason for making the preps this way. Masses of research into the effectiveness of the preparations, since 1924, include attempting to make them in different ways – e.g., putting them into glass containers instead of animal parts. These alternate methods have been shown not to work, they don't produce the intensely potent and effective preparations that the original method does. There is also some unusual and not well known scientific evidence to back up the way the preps are made, such as that done by Lilly Kolisko.

Lilly Kolisko (1893-1976) was perhaps the best pioneer of this sort of research. She tried various ways of making the preparations. For instance, with the oak bark, she wanted to see if it was really necessary to put in into an animal's skull so she placed some in an earthenware pot as well as some in a skull. When she looked at them in the spring, at the end of the preparation time, the oak bark in the skull had become like the living soil whereas that in the earthenware pot was still the same reddish-brown oak bark that she had put into it the previous year, no change at all had come about. She had similar results with her experiments at making all the preparations in different ways – doing them using the animal containers worked, trying to make them in non-animal containers didn't.

In the 1920's, while working on a suggestion made by Rudolf Steiner, Kolisko devised a method for experimentally investigating the workings of the etheric forces in material substance. She called this technique Capillary Dynamolysis and continued to investigate and refine the method until she died. She particularly applied it to researching agriculture, testing composting methods, and investigating disease processes in plants, animals and man. If you Google Capillary Dynamolysis you can find out more about it.

The technique is a beautifully simple, qualitative and repeatable scientific test. During many years of extensive research on Foot and Mouth disease she, and her husband Eugene, developed a thorough picture of it. This supports the findings of Sir Albert Howard that, due to over stimulation, incorrect feeding, one sided breeding and an overall lack of consideration for the animal's true nature. All of which make the organism lose its living connection to the earth and hence its resistance to the virus. We should take all this on board in our current work with animals.

Resonant Communication

When I was a teenager I had boyfriends who were radio hams, though I never dabbled myself, and I remember the old crystal radio sets. As I understood it – which was not in any depth and came out of the attitude "if you can't change them, join them" with the boyfriends – the sets worked on the principle of a vibrating antenna that resonated with another antenna, far away, that was cut to a matching frequency. This wasn't too hard for me as I also had friends who were musicians and had seen/heard a violin string sound when a string of the same frequency on the piano had been plucked. Both the crystal radio and the sounding of the violin string are examples of what is called resonant communication.

Much later, I read about a man called Phillip Callahan who had come to some conclusions based on this resonance that made a difference to how I thought of biodynamics.

Briefly, insect antennae are both receivers and transmitters of infra-red energy. For instance, a male moth's antennae can pick up infra-red signals from the female that tell him where she is and that she is ready to mate. Callahan did a lot of research on the subject – he had been a radio engineer in WWII on the project in Southern Ireland that had used radio beams to guide planes to bomb German ships. His research showed that insects work this way but it was difficult to see how they could because, in order for them to do so, to work with what radio engineers call "long-period antennae", the wavelengths transmitted by the insects would have to be coherent. Coherent means the waves would have to all be in step, like the light from a laser as opposed to the random light from a light bulb. Without this coherency the insect antennae couldn't possibly tune to resonate with each other. It's like how the crystal radio is tuned to your favourite station.

Callahan's discoveries showed that the emissions and the insect antennae were coherent. His research lead to a better understanding of insect communication involving scent and chemical pheromones as well as infra-red. Massive research into the shape of insect antennae, with the aid of the electron microscope, shows that the shapes of the antennae are the same as those developed by radio engineers to pick up similar frequencies. It seems we got it right!

What has this to do with biodynamics? Well, Steiner made some major propositions on antennae and resonance. It's the reason we use cow's horns to make two of the preparations, and the reason we use the stag's bladder to make the Yarrow compost prep, because he said the horns and antlers are a form of antennae for frequencies beyond those we currently understand. The horns and antlers somehow bring beneficial energy into the cow dung, silica and yarrow flowers.

Far fetched as it seems, Callahan's work shows that insects and animals (he worked with animal horns too) actually are antennae from the perspective of the engineer as well as from that of the clairvoyant Steiner. Perhaps Steiner was ahead of his time.

Cosmic Energy

Cosmic energy is energy that comes from outer space, from the cosmos. There's masses of it about, we're involved in it, all the time and it affects us in many ways. One that you probably know about is sun spots; they mess up radio waves, can blow up computers and may be exacerbating global warming. Then there's sunlight itself – without which we wouldn't be here. If somebody turned the sun off we, and Planet Earth, would die in very short order but sunlight, too, is cosmic energy.

Then there's the light from the stars. At a very basic level this light enables us to see them. But light itself is cosmic energy, what we see is the visible part of the electromagnetic spectrum. Visible light is just a tiny little fraction – the rainbow – in the middle of this huge spectrum. The whole electromagnetic spectrum does a lot more to/for us than just ensure we see well enough not to trip over things in the dark. The infra-red I mentioned in the resonant communication section above is an enormous part of it.

We ourselves wouldn't be able to communicate – no mobile phones for instance, no internet "clouds", no radio or TV or GPS satellites – without it. So many of the things we're used to and take for granted couldn't happen without the electromagnetic spectrum, without cosmic energy. Much of it goes right through the planet, and our bodies, as if there was nothing there and it affects us even if we have no idea how it manages to do this, we can see the results.

Some we do know about – cancer patients are treated with radio-active energy to destroy the cancer cells; eyesight can be corrected with laser beams; doctors find out lots about us through X-rays. All of this is using cosmic energy. But there is masses of cosmic energy streaming through us all the time that we have no idea about.

Some of this cosmic energy comes to us from the stars, the constellations. Steiner said it works with the plants and the soil when they are tuned together with the aid of the preparations. We don't know why this happens and only the basics of how – how to make the preps and use them. The fact that we don't know much about it doesn't stop it working, any more than that we still know very little about sun spots stops them having an effect on us, and all our electronic communications, as well as lots of other things.

Our lack of knowledge can have an effect on us, however, making us fearful, and so sceptical. However, being human we can cut off our noses to spite our faces by not working with the little we do know, like biodynamics, because we don't understand it and so are afraid of it. I said at the beginning we don't know why electricity works but that doesn't stop us turning the light switch on and off as we need to. We live quite cheerfully with the paradox of "is light waves or particles?" without having nervous breakdowns. We can work with things we don't understand much about without going nuts ... and working with them often increases our knowledge whereas waiting until we know everything doesn't, in fact it often drastically delays our understanding.

The Engineering Approach

Cosmic energy affects us, however it's transmitted from the constellations, stars and planets. We don't understand very much about it but Biodynamics gives us doable ways of working. That's a very practical engineering approach.

Many years ago I was fortunate enough to meet the Nobel prize-winner and engineer Eric Laithwaite, the man who invented the linear motor and worked all his life with "spin energy", look him up on the web. He was giving a talk at the Society of Mechanical Engineers to which Paul and I went along. We were in exalted but very friendly company ... Lady Finniston, wife of Sir Monty Finniston the then chief government scientist, served me my cup of tea from a wonderful urn that must have been in a NAAFI in WWII.

The talk was very good. I've said before I'm not a scientist, nor an academic, but Laithwaite was so good he put over his ideas without any need to baffle me with mathematics or physics. His basic premise was that engineers "do it" while theoretical physicists "think about it". He began the talk by saying, in his lovely Lancashire accent, "I like talking to school children. I don't like the teachers so much, but I like the children. I usually begin me talk by just standing there, oop front, and dropping me keys from one hand to the other." – he demonstrated for us – "Sooner or later," he went on, " some bright little beggar says, 'Hey! Mister! Why'm you dropping them keys?'. I answers him with 'Because, someday, I'm always hoping they'll go oop.'"

I loved it. A man of that stature who lived right outside the box, who hoped that the laws of physics might one day be set on their head so his keys, instead of falling down, might fly up when he let them go.

He finished his talk in a similar vein, showing us a cartoon of a woman driving a car with Learner-plates. She looks terrified and perplexed – hair standing on end and eyes popping. The young driving instructor, sat beside her, also looks concerned but attempts to calm her. The car itself is flying along some feet above the tops of the trees beside the side of the road, so their panic was understandable! The speech-bubble from the driving instructor's mouth says, "Now then, Mrs. Posstlethwaite, don't you panic. But when we get back down to the ground just you try to remember exactly what it was you did."

The audience loved it. Laithwaite's point was that the instructor, despite not having a clue what was going on, hung onto the possibility that if Mrs. Posstlethwaite could recall what she'd done, just before the car took off, they might be able to repeat the event. He didn't need to understand what had happened before he tried to make it happen again; he realised that understanding might eventually come from the practice-effect, from repeating the event.

I feel that way about biodynamics. I don't know why it works but I do know how to make it happen, time after time.

Science works this way. Somebody comes up with an idea, an event. They try to repeat it and sometimes succeed; they write up what they did to make it happen and keep practising those actions until they're pretty sure they'll work every time. At this point the bright idea is graced with a new name, the theory. The scientist then publishes his or her idea, along with the method, and other scientists try to repeat it. If they succeed, get similar results to the first scientist, then the process becomes established. They all may, still, not know why it works, or fully what it does even, but they know they can do it again, and again, and again. That goes for biodynamics too. We can make the same things happen, the speedier rate of germination by sowing a seed on the relevant day, the increased depth of the topsoil, the more efficient compost that you need to use less of, and the faster compost making process, to name a few effects.

We don't know, or need to know, why it happens, even if we have ideas on the subject, we can still do it again and again and again.

Planets

The planets used in biodynamics are the seven inner ones that have been known for hundred, thousands, of years.

The three outer planets, Neptune, Uranus and Pluto are not yet commonly worked with in biodynamics. Pluto hadn't been discovered when Steiner gave his lectures. People are beginning to look at them but very little has been written up on them as yet.

Steiner worked from a geocentric (Earth-centred) perspective because we live and work on the Earth. Nowadays we call it a Gaia-perspective from James Lovelock's work to help us see life in a holisitc way. It's a convenient way of working, similar to astronomical charts which talk of Jupiter rising and setting for instance. The chart-makers are perfectly well aware that Jupiter doesn't orbit the Earth but it does appear to rise and set to a person standing on the Earth, looking at the sky. All the planets, and the constellations, appear to do this.

Maria Thun uses her own observation work on the planets along with the hints Steiner left about how they might affect plant growth. He suggested the Earth, Moon, Mercury and Venus are to do with reproduction, and that Mars, Jupiter and Saturn are to do with nutrition. The star calendar reflects this. Precisely what the planets do is still under lots of research, we only know a bit so far.

Using the planets is more complicated than just working with the preparations – and it isn't vital to getting a good biodynamic system going in your garden. Get a handle on using the preps with the calendar first, that will give you a good grounding.

The planets help with controlling pests and weeds as well as aiding the growth of plants we want to grow. The ancients assigned various metals to the planets – Google alchemy for more about how they did this. Steiner and his colleagues worked on similar lines, finding that some elements necessary for gardening seem to be aligned with particular planets. Maria Thun and her son, Matthias, are among those researching this so, hopefully, we'll know more as time goes on.

Hugh Courtney, an expert at producing the preparations, views them as a complete system that appears to represent the forces of the solar system as they work with the Earth.

He identifies each prep with a planet.

500: manure – Earth
501: silica – Sun
502 yarrow:– Venus
503: chamomile – Mercury
504: nettle – Mars
505: oak bark – Moon
506: dandelion – Jupiter
507: valerian – Saturn

Courtney postulated that other preps will be found that have the attributes of Neptune, Uranus and Pluto – despite the latter having been relegated to "minor planet" status by current astronomers.

Whether or not you want to go along with these thoughts makes no difference to the efficacy of the preps on the land, on the plants and in the compost heap. As I've said, we really don't have to know why something works to know that it does work. We already do, and use, many things we don't understand all that much of. Take cars for instance, do you know why the spark happens when the electricity jumps between the poles of the spark plug? You know it does happen, you may even have watched it happen, but why? And why does it make a difference how far apart the poles of the spark plug are? Why does the gap in the spark plug have to be adjusted so accurately? Why does that matter? It almost sounds as if the electricity is alive, that it can only jump a particular distance. If the distance is too far it won't make it so it doesn't try, too close and it doesn't bother to jump and make a spark at all.

That "why" question is just so hard to answer, isn't it? But we're still quite happy to use the car despite not understanding why it works. Some of us know how to make it work, but the "why" ... ah! ... there's the question.

Intuition

Many folk scoff at the idea of intuition but they probably use it without realising. Most people have had a feel about something and later discovered how appropriate that feel was. Maybe they followed it up, maybe they didn't and wished they had, but it's a thing people have, even if we can't explain it and there's so much we can't explain.

Steiner said ... The gardener takes note of, and works with, the seasons ... This "taking note" of something is a form of intuition. Part of intuition is about our own wisdom, knowledge, experience and, most of all, how we are able to make connections between these three and come to useful conclusions.

So, try this ... Go sit in your garden, just sit there. Don't try to think, and definitely don't try NOT to think, that's disastrous! It's like if I say "don't think of an elephant for the next five minutes". You're going to sit there, watch in hand, saying to yourself, "Am I thinking of an elephant?" and, of course, you are!

Letting your mind just go with the flow is the best way, they used to call it "reverie", a form of dreaming, day-dreaming perhaps. It lets things come into your mind without being organised by what you expect to see. It works because your thinking, rational mind has gone on hold and you are just allowing yourself to be stimulated by what is around you. This way, the rational mind isn't on duty to censor any thought that doesn't conform with whatever its "comfort box" is, so "unthinkable" thoughts can come in and stir up lots of new ideas and ways of seeing things.

So sit there, in your garden, going with the flow. I try to do this for a few minutes every day. It's worth it. You'll find you notice a lot more about how your garden works with the weather, the time of day, the seasons, the light, the shade, the heat, the cold. And you'll notice things that are different because of other things you've done, like putting the preps on the land or in the heap.

As you get more practiced at doing this you'll find yourself realising things that may have been happening for quite a while but you'd been so "busy" and "in your head" you hadn't been able to see them. You also get more relaxed, less worried that someone may laugh at you for sitting stirring cow-muck for an hour, then getting a paintbrush and flicking it all over the garden. You worry even less as you get used to the beautiful flowers and the fabulous-tasting veg! You relax enough to say, "I really haven't a clue why it works but my own personal experience shows me that it does".

Biodynamics is like that. Our personal experience is what makes things real for us gardeners!

Further Reading & Contacts

I've found these books very interesting and mind-broadening but they are by no means vital to doing biodynamic gardening. If you want to look further, get your head around some new concepts maybe, then these are a good place to start.

Secrets of the Soil by Peter Tomkins & Christopher Bird – This book is excellent, and readable. It's the best I've yet found on the soil and plants and the philosophies behind all this work. The book dates from 1989 and went out of print for a while but is now back. Their book The Secret Life of Plants is also excellent.

The Body Electric by Robert O Becker MD – I like this book; it's very interesting and helped me get to know myself in a different way – this actually helped the gardening too! But it may not be to everyone's taste and is not about gardening!

The Pedrelandra Workbook & Workbook II by Machaelle Small Wright – These books are for when your mind really needs stretching and you feel like going quite whacky and off the wall … but her practices really do work!

The Magic of Findhorn – You may like to read this, it's the book that Machaelle Small Wright off on her own quest. It's about the original foundation of Findhorn. It's not at all like that now up there; it's all full of courses and people trying to get you involved in various (mostly good, if expensive) ways to save the planet. But the original beginning, how it happened with the three founders, is fascinating and fairly mind-blowing … but, again, it really worked and the things they achieved were recorded and very real. These people really walked their talk, and scientifically, even if it seems completely barking.

BD Contacts

Country	Contact
Australia	www.biodynamics.newt.au
Canada	www.demetercanada.com
Ireland	bdaai@indigo.ei & www.demeter.ei
New Zealand	www.biodynamics.org.nz
South Africa	www.bdaasa.org.za
USA	http://www.jpibiodynamics.org
Josephine Porter Institute	& on Facebook
Biodynamic Farming & Gardening Association	www.biodynamics.com
UK: BDA	www.biodynamics.org.uk & on Facebook

BOOKS

Moon Books

PAGANISM & SHAMANISM

What is Paganism? A religion, a spirituality, an alternative belief system, nature worship? You can find support for all these definitions (and many more) in dictionaries, encyclopaedias, and text books of religion, but subscribe to any one and the truth will evade you. Above all Paganism is a creative pursuit, an encounter with reality, an exploration of meaning and an expression of the soul. Druids, Heathens, Wiccans and others, all contribute their insights and literary riches to the Pagan tradition. Moon Books invites you to begin or to deepen your own encounter, right here, right now. If you have enjoyed this book, why not tell other readers by posting a review on your preferred book site. Recent bestsellers from Moon Books are:

Journey to the Dark Goddess
How to Return to Your Soul
Jane Meredith
Discover the powerful secrets of the Dark Goddess and transform your depression, grief and pain into healing and integration.
Paperback: 978-1-84694-677-6 ebook: 978-1-78099-223-5

Shamanic Reiki
Expanded Ways of Working with Universal Life Force Energy
Llyn Roberts, Robert Levy
Shamanism and Reiki are each powerful ways of healing;
together, their power multiplies. *Shamanic Reiki* introduces
techniques to help healers and Reiki practitioners tap ancient
healing wisdom.
Paperback: 978-1-84694-037-8 ebook: 978-1-84694-650-9

Pagan Portals – The Awen Alone
Walking the Path of the Solitary Druid
Joanna van der Hoeven
An introductory guide for the solitary Druid, *The Awen Alone*
will accompany you as you explore, and seek out your own
place within the natural world.
Paperback: 978-1-78279-547-6 ebook: 978-1-78279-546-9

A Kitchen Witch's World of Magical Herbs & Plants
Rachel Patterson
A journey into the magical world of herbs and plants, filled with
magical uses, folklore, history and practical magic. By popular
writer, blogger and kitchen witch, Tansy Firedragon.
Paperback: 978-1-78279-621-3 ebook: 978-1-78279-620-6

Medicine for the Soul
The Complete Book of Shamanic Healing
Ross Heaven
All you will ever need to know about shamanic healing and
how to become your own shaman...
Paperback: 978-1-78099-419-2 ebook: 978-1-78099-420-8

Shaman Pathways – The Druid Shaman
Exploring the Celtic Otherworld
Danu Forest
A practical guide to Celtic shamanism with exercises and
techniques as well as traditional lore for exploring the Celtic
Otherworld.
Paperback: 978-1-78099-615-8 ebook: 978-1-78099-616-5

Traditional Witchcraft for the Woods and Forests
A Witch's Guide to the Woodland with Guided Meditations and
Pathworking
Melusine Draco
A Witch's guide to walking alone in the woods, with guided
meditations and pathworking.
Paperback: 978-1-84694-803-9 ebook: 978-1-84694-804-6

Wild Earth, Wild Soul
A Manual for an Ecstatic Culture
Bill Pfeiffer
Imagine a nature-based culture so alive and so connected,
spreading like wildfire. This book is the first flame...
Paperback: 978-1-78099-187-0 ebook: 978-1-78099-188-7

Naming the Goddess
Trevor Greenfield
Naming the Goddess is written by over eighty adherents and
scholars of Goddess and Goddess Spirituality.
Paperback: 978-1-78279-476-9 ebook: 978-1-78279-475-2

Shapeshifting into Higher Consciousness
Heal and Transform Yourself and Our World with Ancient
Shamanic and Modern Methods
Llyn Roberts
Ancient and modern methods that you can use every day
to transform yourself and make a positive difference in the
world.
Paperback: 978-1-84694-843-5 ebook: 978-1-84694-844-2

**Readers of ebooks can buy or view any of these
bestsellers by clicking on the live link in the title. Most
titles are published in paperback and as an ebook.
Paperbacks are available in traditional bookshops. Both
print and ebook formats are available online.**

**Find more titles and sign up to our readers' newsletter at
http://www.johnhuntpublishing.com/paganism
Follow us on Facebook at
https://www.facebook.com/MoonBooks
and Twitter at https://twitter.com/MoonBooksJHP**